Secret Charms of *Italy*

Introduction
by Vittorio Emiliani

Touring Club of Italy

© 1996 Touring Editore s.r.l. - Milan

Text: Francesco Soletti
Design and editorial concept: Asterisco srl
Editing and layout: Marta Del Zanna,
Fabio Pelliccia
Picture research: Irvana Malabarba
Graphics: Guglielmo Ghizzardi
English translation: Antony Shugaar, New York
(Jan Hardie for the Introduction)

Production*:* Stefano Bagnoli

Printed by Rotolito Lombarda, Pioltello
(Milan, Italy)

Code: G3W
ISBN 88-365-1081-7

To the reader

The fact of having conceived of and published a book offering its readers page upon page of the most fascinating sights and aspects of our Country, does not entail ignoring the fact that other sights and aspects also exist. Those, as Vittorio Emiliani reminds us in his detailed opening essay, due to "the massacre and the wounds inflicted on it, especially during the last half century, by both legal and illegal cement construction work". On the one hand it entails recognizing that the attractions so abundantly spread out in our cities and throughout our countryside do in any case make Italy one of the most visited tourist areas in the world. And on the other hand, it entails coming to the conclusion that it is possible to increase tourist traffic to this area even more: provided that a convinced and integrated rationalization of the tourist system materializes alongside strict protection of the vast environmental and cultural inheritance.

The book is a long and comfortable journey through an at times unknown Italy. And when it touches on a known area, it will be a pleasant surprise to notice parts previously overlooked due to the fact that one's powers of observation had not been sufficiently stimulated. A high interest level is obtained by the constantly beautiful and at times wonderful photographs, also because of the way in which they excite our curiosity with regard to that attractive collective ceremony which is daily life in many places throughout Italy even today. And the texts, ably playing counter-melody to the photographs, help the reader to immerse himself in such varied scenes. They are concise notes bringing the spirit of the different areas into focus. Veneto and its waters, Campania, its art and nature, Sicily and its ancient Mediterranean qualities. They are short tales within the folds of history which has fashioned the many towns, large and small, of the "Bel Paese": from "Savoy" Turin, crowned by the Alps, to "Norman" Palermo, looking out to the Tyrrhenian Sea; from "Lombard" Cividale, within the Friulian hills, to "romantic" Ravello, magical viewpoint on the magical Amalfi coast. If the definition of *charming book* is appropriate to this volume, it is also because serious and impassioned commitment has been lavished on the work for its realization.

Giancarlo Lunati
Touring Club of Italy President

Introduction

"For which many people from far away lands come to see her, not for any need, but for the excellence of arts and crafts, and for the beauty and decoration of the city". In the early years of the 14th century, Dino Compagni, a man of letters and great "chronicler", said this about Florence, but, putting city in the plural, it can, notwithstanding everything, still be said today about Italy and about its countless aspects, urban and agricultural, Alpine and Mediterranean, mountainous and flat, populated and silently deserted. The Bel Paese, the Garden of Europe are still here, despite the massacre and the wounds inflicted on it, especially during the last half century, by both legal and illegal cement construction work.

J. Ruskin, *Courmayeur and the Mont Blanc*.

It is sufficient to look from the Western Alps, the French side from where Hannibal arrived with his procession of elephants and men at arms, in order to come face to face with extraordinarily beautiful valleys and with evidence of that long-ago past, like the Roman bridge at Châtillon, where an even more famous castle rears up, and like the Augustan gate and arch in Aosta. That which Compagni called the "excellence of crafts" is exemplified in the valleys by the very peasant architecture built by skilled "master craftsmen", by the mountain people themselves, some of whom, who knows, may have closely observed the famous "Comacine master builders" at work, those who constructed half of Italy in the Middle Ages. Piedmont is also the land of sanctuaries, of Holy Mounts, such as the one at Varallo which is amongst those most visited, but there are others even more isolated and charming. Amongst the vine and scrub covered hill sides there lie red-brick cities, and Turin stands out from them all, a city completely restructured by a real "royal" architect as was Filippo Juvarra from Messina, who, with the renovated Royal Palace, with the Rivoli Castle, with the Stupinigi Palace, with the Superga Basilica, endowed the city with inextinguishable reference points. It is a very special city, also because of this 18th century lay out it possesses, a city wealthy in museums and art galleries (including the great Egyptian collection, the collection of the House of Savoy and the modern art collection), but it is still mainly ignored by cultural tourism, or, at the very least, underestimated. Perhaps on account of its reserve, for its marginal positioning with respect to the central axis of the country. It is, instead, well worth visiting, understanding, grasping in its essence as a capital (it has also been the capital of cinema, even of radio broadcasting, and it is today's car capital). At the opposite extreme Trieste is, after all, a city with the same destiny, the most "international" of the cities with Italian culture and language, close to a much more

F.M.F. Storelli, *The "Valentino" and the Po River in Turin*.

unstable frontier. In this case as well, the lay out is quite original with respect to the other hundred historical Italian cities: surrounding the inevitable roman monuments, in the course of a few decades (those of the neoclassical period), and due to the political design of Maria Theresa of Austria, a maritime-harbour centre came into being, destined to experience great prosperity, the headquarters of the first shipping companies, of the most active shipyards, and of insurance companies still of primary importance today.

Behind the ports of Trieste and Venice, (which was already in full decline at that period), yet again we find a sobre, determined and mountain dweller Italy: that of the high country wood sculptors, of the parks and of the Dolomite peaks, that which is marked in Friuli by the passage of the Lombards, a people whose origin is still mysterious, protagonist of the period in which the solemn, romanesque churches were erected, from here onwards extending to the entire Po plain. In an even more defensive position, the city of the Bishop-Princes which ruled over a vast alpine territory for decades: Bressanone. With an ecclesiastical museum, situated in the bishop's palace, which is among the very few to relate the social history of the Diocese as well, with a wide range of unusual instructional documentation.

Going down towards the Adriatic Sea, even amidst the signs of recent and intense economic development, is still possible, on the Marano lagoon, to admire the distinctive straw and rush houses also commonly to be found further south, as well as Venice which is known to all, and whose origins are to be looked for during the period of the worst barbarian raids, in the forced emigration of a group of people from Aquileia who erected their beautifully mosaic paved Cathedral, in the centre of one of the most interesting and evocative archaeological areas in the north of the country. We are just a few steps away from the luxurious wealth of Venice and of Veneto, from the villas built by the nobility of the Republic of Venice, using characters called Andrea Palladio and Giambattista Tiepolo (who often worked together here with his son Giandomenico).

A. Dürer, *The Castle of Arco, Trentino.*

C.Ph. Fohr, *Landscape at the Brennero Mountain Pass.*

But the journey through this Italy of large and small capital cities is already moving southwards, towards the plains which, up until the last century, were very rich in fishing waters and marshes, reclaimed at a later date. A landscape still ripe with charm, even from a chromatic view point. For example, on the shores of Lake Garda, there are the red fortified village of Sirmione and the Roman remains calling to mind the birth of Catullus, a poet as transgressive as much as the Mantuan Virgil was official.

Speaking of which, between Mantua and Ferrara, an essential part of the life at court, the history, and the Italian Renaissance art is unfolded. The Gonzaga dynasty of Mantua endured at length and was one of those most involved in that "repre-

6

sentational economy" which probably distanced us from the first industrial revolution, leaving us, however, heirs to an estate which will, for example, renovate the Mantua Ducal Palace and that amazing, playful, rural residence which is Palazzo Te. A city where great and high ranking architects like Leon Battista Alberti and Giulio Romano leave their mark. And nearby, at Sabbioneta, another Gonzaga tried to realize the utopia of his little Athens, with the first real theatre (called "old-fashioned"), permanent and roofed over, constructed by Vincenzo Scamozzi. A still well-conserved jewel.

T. Shotter Boys, *Neptune Place in Bologna.*

In Ferrara a painting school of rare excellence (Cosmè Tura, Ercole Roberti, Francesco del Cossa, and then Dosso, Garofalo and others) is combined with an even greater urban utopia: The "Herculean Addition", directed by Biagio Rossetti. This doubles in size the already beautiful mediaeval city with, in the centre, the mighty Estense Castle and its four great towers. The Po is already broad at Ferrara and it divides up into various branches which a little further ahead will form the Delta, where the stretches of water are broken up by tongues of land covered by reeds or even by treelands. Poplars and, at Mesola, the ancient "Estense delight", holm oaks planted by the lords of Ferrara themselves in the 15 th century, forming that intact Mesola Forest (Boscone della Mesola) which is on occasion invaded peacefully by the sea. Horses and deer, and all varieties of bird species, resident and migratory, may be found here.

Up until the 19th century, it was possible, travelling by water, to reach industrious Bologna, rich, in the same way as Padua and Udine, in canals, mills, and hydraulically powered textile factories. Like other major cities situated along the route of the Roman Via Emilia, from Rimini to Piacenza, Bologna has had a strange destiny. It has in fact conserved, – except unfortunately for the walls – its own historical centre made distinctive by kilometers and kilometers of hospitable red colonnades. Within the area of the centre there are some of the most beautiful churches of the period, beginning with the gothic San Petronio, with the extremely original churches of Santo

E. Lear, *Finale Ligure.*

Stefano and San Domenico which boasts three cloisters. There are richly furnished and varied museums: The Pinacoteca Nazionale (Raffaello, Reni, the three Carracci, Guercino, Crespi, the 14th Century School etc.), the Archaelogical Museum, the Mediaeval Museum and so on. In the same way as the other cities of the area, Bologna is hospitable and friendly. But cultural tourism visitors are still extremely modest in number, as in Piacenza, in Parma, in Modena or in Faenza.

Following the routes of the ancient "salt roads", it is possible to reach the other sea, in the Liguria area. Here, of course, (as is also the case on the Romagnese Riviera), there is no shortage of tourists. The really keen visitors, however, those who, perhaps even in low season, are fascinated by the beauty of the ancient villages, are relatively few in number. Not only alluding to the better known historical centres – like Albenga to the west and Portovenere to the east – but to what may be discovered and re-discovered away from the coast, in the green and silent valleys, scattered with white, pink and grey towns. Reserved in the same way as ducal Genoa, which appears to save its many treasures for itself.

In order to understand how the whole of inland Liguria once was, it is well worth the effort to start off from Portofino and to climb its Mount, a park which is constantly threatened by pyromaniacs and by potential speculators who have never given up hope. Or else to walk along the paths of the practically intact Cinque Terre area, a route through vineyards and terraces which is certainly demanding but which is constantly full of surprises. From up there looking downwards it is possible to glimpse luminous fragments of ancient charm.

G. Zocchi, *View of Florence.*

E. Lear, *The Mount Corno in Abruzzo.*

By means of the Via Francigena and by other roads tramped along by pilgrims, by "romei", (pilgrims bound for Rome), you enter into the heart of Tuscany which is one of the most multi-centred of our regions, dense with city towers bearing witness to a distant, harsh and creative pride: from the towers of San Gimignano, built of brick and of hard stone, high up over the town and over the countryside with its vine and olive clad ridges, to Florence itself which counts its towers and museums by the dozen, (more than sixty, from the enormous Uffizi, to the Foligno Last Supper), to the secluded and fortified Colle di Val d'Elsa, to the other 15th century "urban project", desired by Piccolomini and designed by Bernardo Rossellino: Pienza, miraculously well-balanced and fitted over the already existent mediaeval village. In the same way as from Montalcino and from San Quirico d'Orcia, from these walls it is possible to admire a remote and unusual landscape, the same to be observed behind Guidoriccio da Fogliano in Siena Public Hall: that is to say, a landscape sown with corn and with lesser known cereals, studded by solitary oaks, furrowed by the occasional green tongue or topped by a row of cypress trees. In the same shades which on the painting board bear the name "Siena earth, natural and scorched", or else ocra. A landscape for which, with great difficulty, the first historic-artistic Park was formed.

But this turreted Tuscany is also the land of some of the most important monasteries and of abbeys in the country. Following the above mentioned Via Francigena it is possible to reach Sant'Antimo Abbey, mighty and white in the Montalcino countryside, with proportions calling to mind the Cistercian architecture of France and Lombard architecture, and then, while listening to Vespers or Lauds in Gregorian chanted by these few aristocratic monks, you discover that the teachers of

Sant'Antimo were of French and Lombard origin. Higher up, in mountain woodlands, you come to a Benedictine convent which reached enormous proportions in the 15th century, Monte Oliveto Maggiore in Asciano, with frescoes by Luca Signorelli and by Sodoma, as well as wooden inlays crafted in a manner creating fascinating prospective illusions.

S.J. Ainsley, *Bolsena*.

Tuscany, of course Tuscany, has been discovered to such an extent by the English and by the Germans that the former refer to it as Chiantishire, and the latter boast a "Tuscan" district in the Bundestag. The Marches are an area less well known at the moment, even if Urbino, its Palace-city, and the Art Gallery there with its Piero della Francesa and Paolo Uccello collections, are now famous world wide. Pesaro is less well known, even although it has a later period but harmonious Ducal Palace, esteemed Civic Museums (its masterpiece being the Bellini *Pala dell'Incoronazione*), and an extremely valid ceramic tradition.

Equalling in every way the more inland Urbania, there is ancient Casteldurante, with a third Ducal Palace, where Francesco Maria II stayed, the last of the Della Roveres. Here we once again find mainly uncontaminated countryside, marked by the distinguished web of cities, towns and walled villages, for the most part very well preserved, discretely kept, clean, still inhabited and lived in. A town which stands out for altitude in this region made up of mountains sloping down towards the Adriatic, is certainly Corinaldo, an excellent example of fortification work. Having reached the Abruzzo border at this point, we come to one of the more inland art cities, and perhaps less visited for this reason: Ascoli Piceno with its great, harmonious square on a level with those of Vigevano and of Venice. A particularly fascinating historical centre: here we find especially 16th century Renaissance, and it bears the signature of a painter and architect of Roman origin, Cola dell'Amatrice, who, especially in his second role, competes with the original Ascoli beauty, fusing his work with the solemn, mediaeval structures which were already in existence.

A. Rosengarten, *The Forum in Pompeii*.

Marches and Abruzzo are connected to one another by a green chain of Apennines parks, promoted to the dignified range of National Parks. The joining element is manifested in the still recent Gran Sasso and Monti della Laga National Park, but on the Marches side the Monti Sibillini National Park has been in existence for some years, and on the Abruzzo side there is the park which is, together with Gran Paradiso, the oldest of the National Parks, and which was established by Benedetto Croce, the greatest 20th century Italian philosopher, who was born in Pescasseroli, his mother's home town. In that year of 1922 Croce was head of the Ministry for Public Education, in whose sphere of influence the so-called "natural beauties" fell. It is indeed possible to state today that, thanks to the courageous and advanced work

9

carried out since 1969 by its director Franco Tassi, the Abruzzo National Park is certainly the most successful example of a large protected area (which merits having more attention to it by a State which instead does not fully consider it part of the family). As demonstrated by the by now 2 million annual visitors and the economic activity indirectly generated by the Park Organization now headed by Fulco Pratesi.

J.H. Schilbach, *Seashore near Amalfi.*

If Abruzzo, with its parks, is the greenest of Italy's regions, Umbria has been calling itself green for some time. There are amazing co-existing civilizations here, starting with the Etruscans and with the Romans, who, after all, were the first to organize the region's water in a rational manner and who laid the cities' foundations, from the Gubbio amphitheatre and the one at Spoleto, to the turreted gate at Spello, to Perugia, the major historical centre, rich in monuments and museums, and so well "pedestrianized". A co-existence of different ethnic groups and also of different abilities: in fact, Umbria is the mother land of and the first place of mission work for saints such as Francesco d'Assisi, Benedetto da Norcia, Chiara di Assisi, Rita da Cascia. Umbria is, however, also the mother land of commanders, of the most popular military men: Braccio da Montone, named after whom there is a school, a method of combat, "braccesco", based on violent attack, as opposed to the "sforzesco" method, more tactical and delaying, Erasmo da Narni, known as the Gattamelata – Honeycat – on account of his astuteness, and Niccolò Piccinino of Perugia, who succeeded Braccio at the command of his "lance" (lancers). This region as well is extremely rich in historical centres and in well organized local museums.

It is impossible to speak about the Bel Paese without mentioning Rome, with its three hundred churches and basilicas, with its more than one hundred museums and collections, with the largest historical centre in the world. But, for once, we can take some time to talk about the areas surrounding the Capital. From a naturalistic point of view they are among the most delightful in Italy, in the direction of the Roman Etruria, in the volcanic lakes area, towards Tivoli, in the famous Castelli or in the incredible Ninfa oasis. Nature and landscape are embellished by villages rising above remote Etruscan necropolises, and by "man made" additions like the great papal, cardinal and noble villas, with gardens and ornamental water works, or by constructions bearing the architect's signature in the inhabited areas themselves, like, for example, in Caprarola signed by Vignola.

These remarks may well be repeated with regard to Naples and to its Vesuvian Villas, real marvels, worthy of a cultural capital which we are now re-discovering with the newly-opened Capodimonte Palace, the at long last renovated churches along the *decumanus*, the enormous Plebiscite Square liberated from the assault of cars. The surrounding areas here remain extraordinary, despite the garish ugliness of the last decades. Pompeii, which archaeologists hasten to assure us was merely

C. Gore, *The Concordia Temple in Agrigento.*

one of the provincial imperial cities, although certainly a precious one, but which boasts the unique role of having been conserved for centuries beneath ashes and lapillus, in such a way that it can relate to us how a city of the Roman world really was, without having undergone any further modification.

Puglia extends out on to the other seas, Puglia with its white, Mediterranean villages, the endless series of Romanesque cathedrals, the imposing castles, high above the countryside like the Frederick Castel del Monte or in the heart of the city like the svevian one in Bari, and the at times no less charming fortified estates reflecting arab influence. There is everything in the great Puglia, from dolmens to the baroque (very abundant in Lecce and in Martina Franca). Then you immediately fall back under the spell of the rocky cities and of their frescoed churches, in Massafra, and, in the adjacent Basilicata, in Matera.

Between the coast and the first hills, however, you already perceive the influence of Ancient Greece, of the civilization brought to Metaponto or to Policoro by the *nóstoi*, by the legendary survivors of the Trojan war. Theatres, amphitheatres, acropolises, museums, succeed one another here, in small islands like Lipari and in the great Sicily. A stage acted on by warriors like those made from bronze which were found in the sea in front of Riace in Calabria, and which are now on display in the Reggio National Museum.

E. Lear, *Palermo.*

The experiences and emotions in Sicily are endless, even in the threatened and defaced Valley of Temples in Agrigento, in Segesta, in Selinunte. Greek Sicily, Arab Sicily, Norman Sicily: the kings of this last historical period summoned architects, artists and master craftsmen from overseas to Palermo, in order to build the Zisa, the Cuba and other major constructions.

To conclude this rapid journey through Italy we come to Sardinia, more of an island than Sicily, with oasis which are still amazing nowadays, and a most unusual land and sea fauna and flora. But there are Sardinian riches, in fact, which are as yet little known and under-exploited: archaeological riches, no longer simply isolated "nuraghi", but complete villages like the inland Barumini. Long ago lives, remote, but already intensely creative, quite a long time previous to the arrival of Phoenicians and Carthaginians. "Many people from far away lands come to see her" this beautiful Italy, "for the excellence of arts and crafts" as the Florentine Dino Compagni wrote in his *Chronicle* in the early years of the 14th century. But we should be the first to go and see her, her churches and abbeys, her museums, her historical centres, her castles and convents, her archaeological sites. And we very seldom do. We should be the first to do so, and we should love her, much more than we have done in recent years.

Vittorio Emiliani

Contents

From Alpine Peaks to the Valleys of the Piedmont

From Alpine Peaks to the Valleys of the Piedmont

 In the Middle Ages, two great roads crossed the western Alps, linking the Mediterranean world with northern Europe. The northernmost of the two routes crossed over the Great Saint Bernard Pass, running through the Valle d'Aosta and down into Lombardy; the southern route ran by the Moncenisio, or, in a variant, by the Monginevrino, and down the Val di Susa into Liguria. Just before the year 1000, Sigeric, a newly named archbishop of Canterbury on his way to Rome for his investiture, travelled along the northern route. He left us an invaluable detailed account of his travels. The route he described was one used every year by thousands of pilgrims; over the centuries that followed, it became the main trade route linking Europe's two richest regions, Tuscany and Flanders. Upon reaching the high Alpine pass, probably after a night's rest in the hospice run there by Benedictine monks, Sigeric started down the Gallic consular road, even then a thousand years old, that led straight to the city of Aosta.

Aosta, originally a Roman colony, still has major Roman monuments as well as relics from its prosperous period in the Middle Ages. Among the Roman structures, note the Praetorian Gate, the Arch of Augustus, the forum, the theatre, and a stone bridge over the river Buthier; from mediaeval times, note the collegiate church of Sant'Orso, the cathedral of San Giovanni Battista (St John the Baptist), and the tower of Bramafam.

After Aosta, the scene that unfolded before the eyes of a wayfarer heading down to the Po valley must have been much as it is today. An Alpine valley, shaped by the rushing waters of the river Dora Baltea, fed by immense

Alpine glaciers; a fertile landscape of vineyards, farmland, and pasturage, dotted with country villages and under the watch and ward of numerous castles.

The first castle a wayfarer in the 12th century would have seen was the

Castello di Quart, set in a forbidding, solitary landscape; originally built in 1185, and extensively renovated in later centuries. Then, after Saint-Marcel and Pontey, our wayfarer would have passed the Castello di Fénis, a distinctive mediaeval fortress, with a double ring of walls, immense towers, and ramparts bristling with battlements. After Châtillon and Saint-Vincent, a spa renowned for its hot springs, is the Castello di Verrès, vast and stern, dominating the road below from high atop a rocky crag. Not far off is the Castello di Issogne, a splendid example of a fortified home, richly furnished and frescoed. Still further ahead is the last and most impressive of all, the fortress

Alpine summits of the Valle d'Aosta (preceding pages).

Flocks grazing on lowland pastures.

A mountain church set amidst the evergreens.

If a traveller should be tired of historical landmarks at this point, and if that traveller should wish to breathe some fresh air and visit some of the lesser known corners of Piedmont or Valle d'Aosta, places that have been tucked away out of the mainstream of history for centuries: one such place is the Valsesia, for centuries a cultural island, with its own customs and folkways. Before reaching the snowy expanse of Monte Rosa, of course, our modern wayfarer will have to tolerate a climb studded with remarkable monuments, foremost among them the Sacro Monte di Varallo, one of Italy's most noteworthy sanctuaries.

Vernacular architecture dots the Alpine slopes, often buried under the snow.

The Sacra di San Michele stands high atop a rocky crag, surveying the Valle di Susa far below.

The cloister of Sant'Orso in Aosta, one of the notable monuments of this mountain capital.

of Bard, built in the 11th century as a customs house, enlarged and reinforced repeatedly over the centuries, stout veteran of battles and sieges.

Once our wayfarer reached the valley floor, he would have a choice of directions. The road forked here, heading SE to Ivrea and Vercelli, with their remarkable mediaeval monuments, or SW toward Turin, where the road linked up with the route over the Moncenisio.

The Moncenisio road, after passing through Susa, a town rich in Roman and mediaeval monuments, ran down through the Valle di Susa and, within sight of the plains beyond, ran beneath the towering and noteworthy abbey of Chiusa, also known as the Sacra di San Michele, set high on the summit of a rocky spur. From here, Turin was a short distance; the city boasted dozens of inns and hostels, source of much of its fortune.

Turin is best known to history as the former capital of the House of Savoy, as well as being the hotbed of political and ideological forces that led to the Risorgimento and the Unification of Italy in the 1860s. Turin is a modern city, the product of an orderly city grid and an overall urban plan that, beginning in the 16th century, endowed it with large handsome squares, countless parks, and long, broad, tree-lined boulevards. There are many fine views of the surrounding hills and mountains, Alps to the NW, hills to the SE, beyond the river Po. The hill country to the SE is particularly dear to the people of Turin, and it boasts many villas and great estates. It is not well known to most visitors, however. Even though the suburbs of Turin increasingly encroach upon the hill country, you can still find exquisite landscapes and fine monuments, such as the 18th-century Basilica di Superga, or little Gothic gems such as the town of Chieri.

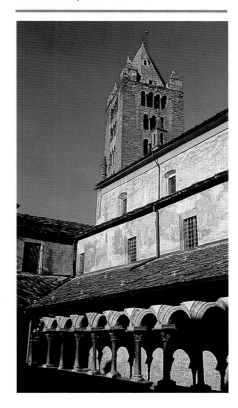

A Bird's-Eye View of Mont Blanc

The first glimpse of Mont Blanc, whether from Italian Courmayeur or from French Chamonix, is an unforgettable and spectacular sight. The mountain juts up sharply, 3,000 metres of ice and snow, like some Himalayan colossus. Its various peaks are often shrouded in clouds that only emphasize its vast mass. Goethe and Chateaubriand hailed Mont Blanc as a phenomenon of nature; the poet Shelley immortalized it in an ode; the Italian Nobel laureate Carducci sang its praises. This is the highest point in

At first, only a few hardy daredevils dared to venture onto the slopes of Mont Blanc, or to scale its towering peaks. The first to reach its summit, in 1786, was a French physician named Michel-Gabriel Paccard. After him came other Romantic adventurers, often accompanied by Alpine guides, secretaries, servants, and intrepid ladies, making their clumsy way across the great sea of ice. They in turn brought a small army of landscape artists and pioneering nature photographers. Nowadays, virtually

all Europe (4,807 m) and for over two centuries travellers and sightseers have converged here from every corner of the continent to admire the mountain's sheer pinnacles, jagged ridges, and high valleys that groan under the weight of broad, twisting glaciers. A circular route (the Tour du Mont-Blanc) has been a mountaineer's classic from the outset; along it, those in search of the sublime and the spectacular have admired the varied slopes of this great Cathedral of Nature, 40 kilometres in length and varying in breadth, from 8 to 15 kilometres.

anyone can enjoy the experience by simply boarding the gondola that runs 15 lofty kilometres, from Entrèves (1,370 m) to the Aiguille du Midi (3,843 m) and Chamonix (1,270 m). In less than an hour, the gondola soars sharply up from the valley floor, carved out in remote ages by ponderous glaciers, and climbs quickly to the lofty gallery of granite pinnacles, shaped by fissuring granite and relentless erosion. The gondola then passes beneath the majestic summit, and on over the awesome glaciers, split by yawning crevasses and notched with immense

seracs. There are many who wish to protect this setting of pristine loveliness from the incursions of builders and developers; their goal is to designate the entire massif as an international natural park.

The Mer de Glace, or "sea of ice," near Chamonix, one of the traditional destinations in the crossing of Mont Blanc (facing page).

The powerful thrusting force of glaciers gouges out mighty boulders, creating settings of incomparable beauty.

Fortresses That Turn into Sumptuous Mansions

Valle d'Aosta is understandably proud of its many castles. All told, there are 130 of them, built to protect the old trade route leading over the Alps. Most of these castles belonged to one of the leading families of Savoy, the Challant. Like their feudal lords, the House of Savoy, the Challant devoted themselves greatly to building. At first they erected doughty military fortifications; over the course of generations, the forts they built came to look more and more like luxurious homes.

A renowned example from the early

or baronial hall, with its fine fireplace and period furniture; the chapel with lovely Gothic frescoes; and the kitchen, with its broad hearth and great display of pewter.

A smaller castle, closer to a townhouse in style, is the Castello di Verrès. Built between 1360 and 1390, it is large, square, and austere; it has no towers. Inside, the vast halls with monumental fireplaces were home to chatelains and the soldiers of the garrison; a remarkable stairway girds all four sides of the courtyard.

family, anxious to be remembered by posterity. The castle is a composite work of art, created by artists from the Po valley and from beyond the Alps, summoned by Giorgio di Challant, a great patron of European culture. Beginning in the 17th century, with the decline of the aristocracy, these and many other castles fell into ruin or were transformed into large farmhouses. The Castello di Fénis, for instance, had hay stacked against its frescoes, while the ground floor was turned into stables. A few noble souls were responsible for

period is the Castello di Fénis, built between 1337 and 1340. Ostensibly, this is a typical mediaeval fortress; it has massive walls, mighty towers, and all the defensive apparatus that its owner, Aimone di Challant, had admired in France. Behind this costly display of military might, however, a stately home is concealed.

You become aware of this as soon as you enter the courtyard, where the double loggia with wooden railings and the frescoed walls create a sophisticated and spectacular effect. The impression is heightened inside, atop the circular staircase that leads to the upper floors. To name a few, note the Sala Baronale,

At Carnival, historical pageants are held, with processions and festivities. Lastly, let us consider the Castello di Issogne, the forerunner of magnificent homes that blended Gothic and Renaissance styles. Built in 1480, it is a vast, rectangular structure, with corner towers and distinctive chimneys. Inside is an exquisite home, adorned with paintings; note the sumptuous baronial hall. Outside, the frescoed entrance hall features frescoes depicting town shops, a rare document of social history. In the courtyard is a lovely fountain shaped like a pomegranate; overhead are the heraldic crests of the leading members of the Challant

saving Valle d'Aosta's castles from certain neglect and destruction; they not only studied the castle architecture and acquainted the rest of the world with them, but they often paid out of their own pockets for their restoration.

The Castello di Fénis is an impressive work of fortification, in which the defensive function determines the architectural form (facing page).

The style of the Castello di Verrès is clearly of urban derivation.

Detail of the frescoes of the Castello di Issogne and the exterior blind arcades.

The Walser Traditions of Alagna Valsesia

In the 13th century settlers of
Germanic stock migrated into the
valleys south of Monte Rosa: they were
called the Walser, because they had
originally come from the Valais canton,
in Switzerland. They were hardy
folk, accustomed to survival in an
unforgiving environment; they were
also tenacious upholders of their
own traditions and folkways. Those
traditions constituted a wind of change
in the secluded mountain valleys
of Piedmont and Valle d'Aosta.
One of the most notable signs of
their colonizing influence – aside
from their Germanic dialect in a world
of Romance languages – was the

A typical home in Alagna (facing page).

The museum-home of the Walser, where the
traditions of a borderland are preserved.

Wood is the prevailing material in the
furnishings.

A vest, from a woman's outfit, made in this
town on the slopes of Monte Rosa.

introduction of central European
building techniques, featuring load-
bearing structures made of stacked
beams, notched at the corners.
In time, the wooden-beam houses
of the Walser began to incorporate
the stone structures typical of the
Roman and Mediterranean world.
Walser homes eventually evolved
into a remarkable synthesis of the
two architectural traditions, providing
structures perfectly suited to the harsh
climate and the needs of an economy
based on farming and livestock. They
were made mostly of larch, with a
stone foundation; stalls occupied the
ground floor, sometimes side-by-side
with the winter sitting room, where
women would gather doing needlework
while the men sang songs or recounted
old tales and legends. Upstairs were
the living quarters proper, lit and
ventilated by a few small windows –
especially scarce on the wall exposed
to the harsh north mountain winds.
Beneath the roof was the hayloft,
which provided insulation from
the winter chill. The south wall had
balconies for drying the harvest
in the summer and autumn sun.
The roof was steeply pitched, so
that snow would slide off.
After many centuries, the Walser
presence in the valleys around Monte
Rosa has dwindled; there are still areas,
however, where the dialect is clearly
Germanic, where the surnames are
distinctly Walser, where the old ways
are still followed. One such place is
Alagna, in the high Valsesia; the town
welcomes tourists, but stubbornly hews
to its cultural identity. The proof is in
the fascinating Walser Museum, with
its large collection of objects eloquent
of a venerable culture that went into
the making of modern Europe.

23

Faith Meets Art on the Sacro Monte of Varallo

A promenade climbing along a hillside to a religious sanctuary; lined with a series of chapels, each decked with frescoes or crowded with sculptures, inspired by mysteries of the Faith or episodes from the life of Christ. This remarkable walkway is meant as a spiritual pilgrimage toward Salvation, allowing each pilgrim to pause and ponder Biblical scenes, in a setting favourable to the uplift of mind and soul. This, in brief, is a "sacro monte," or "holy mount," a unique and typically North Italian religious park, a blend of the mediaeval custom of building symbolic copies of famous holy places with the theological concept of the Stations of the Cross as necessary steps on the path to salvation.

Peculiar to Lombardy and Piedmont, the "sacro monte" was especially popular during the Counter Reformation, when the Church encouraged the construction of sanctuaries as bastions of Roman Catholicism in areas beset by Protestant influence. Indeed, the Church encouraged the veneration of holy images, abhorred by Protestant reformers, as a way of reaffirming the True Faith. Thus, a "sacro monte" became a context in which to portray the phases of Salvation in a way that would stir the soul of a visitor.

The Sacro Monte of Varallo is one of the oldest and largest of its kind. It comprises the Basilica of the Assumption and 44 chapels, adorned with some 600 life-sized statues and 4,000 frescoed figures. Undertaken well before either Reformation or Counter Reformation

in the late-1400s by a Milanese Friar Minor named Bernardino Caimi, the "sacro monte" was a result of Caimi's pilgrimage to the Holy Land in 1481. Work on the enormous project continued for two full centuries, into the early 1700s. The impact and variety of the scenes portrayed are astonishing: certain chapels are crowded with dozens of life-sized posed figures.

Note the grieving mother in the *Slaughter of the Innocents*, clearly a farm girl from the surrounding Valsesia; the toothless and goitered tormenter in the *Ascent to Calvary*, similar to so many inhabitants of the high Alpine valleys; the Roman centurion of the *Crucifixion*, with the features of a Renaissance condottiere. A rogue's gallery of real-life portraits, the creation of a small army of sculptors and painters, the Sacro Monte of Varallo was, and remains, both an anthropological atlas of the Valsesia and a gallery of the valley's finest artists.

Moreover, it is one more example of the way in which holy art and theatrical performance merged in Northern Italy.

Striking gestures of faith and emotion enliven the figures in the 44 chapels of the enormous monumental complex of the Sacro Monte (facing page, and above).

The Piazza dei Tribunali, with four chapels depicting episodes from the life of Christ.

25

In Turin, Challenging the Skills of the Architects

In the second half of the 16th century, the House of Savoy, having made Turin the capital of its dukedom, embarked upon a great rebuilding project that, in the course of the ensuing three centuries, would shape a city worthy of its brief stint as the capital of Italy. During this period, as the Baroque made way for the Neoclassical, more than one great architect emerged. Perhaps the first was an abbot named Guarino Guarini, who designed and built buildings here from 1666 until 1681. Guarini was nicknamed "the mathematician of Baroque" for his remarkable propensity for calculations. He built daring structures, such as the dome of the church of San Lorenzo, and the chapel of the Sacra Sindone, which holds the Shroud of Turin; in the latter, the load-bearing structures almost seem to be on display. He wrote a book on geometry and architecture, at the same time lauding Gothic architecture.

Next came Filippo Juvarra, the leading architectural mind of the early 18th century, whose work developed between two opposite extremes: from the Classicism of the Basilica di Superga to the Baroque of the church

of the Carmine and the facade of the immense, unfinished Palazzo Madama. Carrying on the banners of Guarini and Juvarra to the dawn of the Neoclassical period was Bernardo Antonio Vittone, who drew on their teachings to develop his own unique style of Baroque, which can be seen in the churches of Santa Chiara, San Francesco, and Santa Maria di Piazza. A contemporary of Vittone who was already moving toward Neoclassicism was Benedetto Alfieri, who designed the handsome facade of the Teatro Regio. In the first half of the 19th century, a noble, restrained form of Neoclassical architecture flourished in Turin; it resulted in many lovely homes and mansions. But the real hero of Turin for that century, and one of Europe's and Italy's finest architects, was Alessandro Antonelli. His masterpiece, the immense "Mole Antonelliana" is a remarkable piece of engineering, using traditional materials in a prodigious play of forces and thrusts.

The "Mole," symbol of Turin (facing page).

The exterior of Palazzo Madama (left), a building with sumptuous interiors (below).

A view looking up at the dome of the church of San Lorenzo, by Guarino Guarini.

27

The Magic of the Dolomites

Déodat de Dolomieu (1750-1801) was a prominent French geologist and mineralogist, but little would be remembered of his life and academic career, however adventurous and fruitful, had he not given his name to the mineral "dolomite," and thereby to the lovely range of mountains where that mineral is chiefly found, the Dolomites.

and Trentino-Alto Adige, diligently listing the valleys that form its boundaries. Others refer more generally to the natural characteristics of these mountains, found in large, isolated massifs or groups, of moderate elevation (around 3,000 m), with relatively little perennial snow, and shaped by erosion into fantastic shapes. Yet others define the Dolomites as the region inhabited by those belonging to the Rhaeto-Romanic language group, with their distinctive and ancient

customs and folkways. Perhaps it is best to consider the Dolomites as a combination of all of these; in any case, we tend to think primarily of single peaks linked to great feats of the golden age of mountaineering.

Even to list the names of places that have made the Dolomites famous is a daunting task. Still, having to provide a partial and inadequate list, and being forced to leave out some deserving

Who can say whether, during a fateful research expedition in 1791, Dolomieu was more moved at the spectacular mountain landscape or excited at having discovered a new mineral, a particularly magnesium-rich limestone? Certainly, a traveller would have to vote for the view. Immense rock walls, mighty spires and towers, delicately serrated ridges and crests, and endless highlands, an intricate interplay of vertical and horizontal lines, nuanced by the shades of pink, now a pale rose, there a vivid flush, verging at dawn and dusk into reds and purples, hues most intense just when the valleys are about to be plunged into darkness, or as they emerge from darkness. It is difficult to define with precision the geographical expanse of the Dolomites. Some geographers apply the name to the broad rectangular area south of the Austrian border, encompassing the regions of Veneto

The Valle di Funes (facing pages).

Fin de siècle architecture in Merano, and the 15th-century facade of the Palazzo Assessorile in Cles (above).

Capo di Federa, near Cortina.

names, let us begin with the majestic Sella massif, one of the most spectacular tableaux in the central Dolomites. Extending from the west up toward the Sella is the Val Gardena

(Grödnertal), with its broad meadows and tree-lined slopes. This great valley has some of the best ski resorts in the Dolomites, such as Ortisei (Sankt Ulrich), famous for its traditional wood carvings and fast ski runs. To the south is another treasure trove of mountain beauty, the Alpe di Siusi, a vast Alpine upland covered with meadows and pine forests, enclosed by the mighty massifs of the Sasso Lungo, the Catinaccio, and the Sciliar. Extending from the north up toward the Sella is the less popular but equally notable Val Badia (Gadertal), ending in the Corvara basin. At the base of the Sella's southern slope is Canazei, the chief base camp

The little Alpine church of San Valentino, on the Alpe di Siusi, with its distinctive onion-dome bell tower.

The mountain of Ortles catches one's eye as one surveys the horizon of the Parco Nazionale dello Stelvio.

In the villages of the Val Badia, frescoes by local artists adorn the facades of the houses.

for expeditions up to the massif of the Marmolada. Another notable beauty spot is the fashionable resort town of Cortina d'Ampezzo, in Veneto, one of the most renowned resort areas

in the Cadore region. Here, the Grande Strada delle Dolomiti (Great Road of the Dolomiti), beginning in Bolzano, intersects with the Strada d'Alemagna, running from Venice up to Innsbruck. Surrounded by the summits of the Tofana, the Pomagagnon, the Cristallo, the Sorapis, and the Croda da Lago, this resort area was first discovered by wealthy holiday-makers in the mid-18th century, when the first major luxury hotels were built. It became a popular resort between the World Wars, however, with the first cableways, and more fully in 1956, when Cortina d'Ampezzo hosted the Winter Olympics. Lastly, there is the remarkable massif of the Brenta, marking

the western boundary of the Dolomites; note the remarkable blend of the twisted shapes and rich hues of the Dolomites with the spectacular crystalline grandeur of the central Alps. The pristine forests here are one of the last habitats of the European brown bear as well as other species of Alpine wildlife.

We should also mention a few other names: Bolzano (Bozen), the capital of Alto Adige (Südtirol), the point where the Germanic and Mediterranean worlds are said to meet, with a strong Gothic flavour; Bressanone (Brixen), with its remarkable mingling of mediaeval severity, Renaissance harmony, and Baroque extravagance. To indicate the last few delights of the Dolomites, consider Brunico (Bruneck), the chief town of the Val Pusteria (Pustertal); Merano (Meran), where the Val Passiria (Passeiertal) meets the Adige valley, well watered and abounding in vineyards. So much remains, that an entire book would not suffice.

Bressanone, the Realm of the Bishop-Princes

Bressanone (Brixen in German) is a mountain town with a history of pageant and splendour, revolving chiefly around the courts of the bishop-princes, high prelates who were named princes of the Holy Roman Empire in 1027. These ecclesiastical monarchs thus governed the counties of the rivers Isarco and Inn, ruling over the lands between Bolzano (Bozen in German) and Innsbruck, along the strategic road over the Brenner Pass. These powerful men fashioned the artistic, cultural, and spiritual unity that marked the history of the Tyrol region for so many centuries. A notable product of their wealth and power is the city of Bressanone. Within the circle of mediaeval walls, long since torn down, is a town of riches and tradition, a town of proud monuments, continually embellished and enlarged over the centuries. Of particular interest, in the centre of Bressanone, are the two strongholds of the bishop-princes' ecclesiastical and secular domains: the Cathedral, symbol of spiritual power, and the fortified palace, their residence and the symbol of temporal power. The baroque facade of the Cathedral foreshadows the splendid interior, but it does not prepare you for the succession of two more churches, decorated with fine frescoes, and a Romanesque cloister adorned with vivid frescoes of Bible stories. Equally astonishing is the interior of the stern Palace of the Bishop-Princes, on the far side of the cathedral square. The building is flanked by a massive fortified tower and surrounded by a deep moat. Once inside, however, the visitor is greeted first by a graceful courtyard with a portico topped by two stories of loggia; then by a series of magnificent halls, lavishly adorned

with frescoes and magnificent furnishings. The building also houses the collection of the Diocesan Museum. This impressive display of wealth is matched by the restrained opulence of Bressanone's other buildings. A stroll along the Via Portici Maggiori, lined by handsome homes in a Northern European style, and onto the square before the Gothic parish church of San Michele, shows clearly how Bressanone has prospered from its strategic location on the road over the Brenner Pass, once used by emperors and wealthy merchants; and even now the source of considerable trade.

Cathedral of Bressanone: Frescoes in the vaults of the cloister (facing page).

Stern gestures and silent power emanate from the statues (top) that adorn the Palace of the Bishop-Princes (left).

The sign of the oldest and best-known hotel in Bressanone, a city with long traditions of hospitality.

The Grande Strada, a Road Across the Dolomites

The Grande Strada delle Dolomiti, or the "Great Road of the Dolomites" is easily one of the most spectacular drives on earth. It runs east-west for 109 kilometres, crossing most of the range of the Dolomites, and offering views of breathtaking beauty and magnificence. It links Bolzano (Bozen) to the west with Cortina d'Ampezzo, to the east. This "Great Road" was built, in stages, from 1895 to 1909; it has been greatly improved in recent decades, so that many of the dauntingly steep grades have been replaced with more gradual switchbacks.

The ribbon of asphalt leaves Bolzano, capital of Alto Adige, and enters the Val d'Ega (Eggental), at first a dramatic cut through reddish rock, and later a broad green river valley. The long winding climb runs past the base of the Latemar (2,842 m), a mountain that rises above dense forests of conifers, bristling with jagged pinnacles of grey rock, contrasting in colour with the pinkish hue of most other massifs in the Dolomites. The road plunges into the forest until it reaches the tiny lake of Carezza (Karersee, 1,519 m), a sudden apparition. Soon after, you will reach the pass of Costalunga (Karerpaß, 1,745 m), a broad grassy saddle with a vast panoramic view of mountain peaks, near and far. You then drive down through the broad, verdant Valle di Fassa, framed amidst the high silhouettes of the Sasso Lungo, the Sella, and the Marmolada. Soon after, you will reach Vigo di Fassa; from here, you can explore the Catinaccio group (2,981 m), the most easily accessible massif in the Dolomites and one of the loveliest, a place of uncanny colours at sunrise and sunset; legends and fairy-tales tell of enchanted palaces and witches' sabbaths high among the rock formations. Drive up the valley road and you will reach Canazei, surrounded by majestic peaks, and then the Pordoi Pass (2,239 m), the highest and most spectacular pass in the Dolomites. This marks the beginning of the Livinallongo, and then descends through Arabba, at the foot of the Sella, and around the Col di Lana (2,452 m), the scene of heavy fighting in World War I. At Andraz, the road climbs sharply toward the Falzarego Pass (2,105 m), the last natural obstacle before the final stretch of the Grande Strada delle Dolomiti. Then the road runs past the base of the lovely Tofana di Rozes, down to Pocol, and then on to the verdant mountain hollow of Cortina d'Ampezzo, a world-renowned ski resort and a fitting conclusion to a fine mountain drive.

In the waterfall of Stanga, water erodes and shapes the mountain (facing page).

Beneath the "Gothic" spires of the Latemar, evergreens seem to stand bowed in prayer.

Iridescent colours along the Sasso Lungo and the Tofane, in the early light of dawn.

The Idyllic World of the Alpe di Siusi

A natural terrace 2,000 metres high at the western edge of the Dolomites, 5,000 hectares of Alpine meadows crowned by the Sasso Lungo and the Sciliar, where livestock is let loose to graze from June until the end of August, and where twice each season the valley folk climb up to mow hay – this, in geographical and purely practical terms, is the Alpe di Siusi (Seiser Alm), which recently became a paradise for summer and winter holiday-makers. All the rest is splendid ornamentation, the things that have made life worth living for generations of holiday-makers: the blooming mountain flowers of early summer, the dense stands of trees, chamoix and golden eagles, the panoramic views to the west, overlooking the Valle dell'Isarco, and to the north, over the Val Gardena. This is a world that for many centuries was completely separate, and despite the inevitable modernization, it is still a world that jealously preserves its identity and its traditions: you can sense it in the wooden houses that constitute the ancient town centres, in the traditional dress that still worn for festive occasions, and in the symbolic motifs used in traditional wood carvings. At the end of the only road running through here is the town of Castelrotto (Kastelruth), the oldest settlement in the area, with a dual personality: part Alpine village, with dignified houses clustered around the church – with its tall bell tower – in the centre, and part thriving ski resort, with mountain trails and lifts running up the slopes. The same is true of Selva (Wolkenstein), Santa Cristina, and Ortisei (Sankt Ulrich), renowned places in the Val Gardena. For these towns, the Alpe di Siusi represents the entryway to the true heart of the Dolomites, the section that still resists the "siren song" of modern consumer society. As you hike the trails and ski the snowy slopes, so far away from the noises of everyday life, you enter another world – at first the silence and the enormous spaces may be bewildering, but that sensation quickly passes, and you are soon aware of just how pleasant this place can be. You have the feeling that you have entered a sanctuary, where the presence of humans is evident, but in perfect harmony with nature, a nature that forces you to leave the worries of city life far behind.

Window of a craftsman in Ortisei (facing page).

The Sciliar looms over the Alpe di Siusi.

A wedding in folk costume: Alto Adige is a land of powerful traditions.

The town of Siusi, spreading out on the gently rolling meadows of a romantic and uncontaminated setting.

The Strongholds of a Borderland

The region of Trentino-Alto Adige boasts hundreds of military fortifications dating from the high Middle Ages to the Renaissance, and including fortresses, castles, and watchtowers. Built to defend roads that, since Roman times, have run up the valleys of the rivers Adige and Isarco to cross the Alps at, respectively, the Resia Pass (Reschenpaß in German) and the Brenner Pass (Brennerpaß), the oldest of these forts and castles stand near the region's chief towns: Trent and Bolzano (Bozen) to the south, Merano (Meran) and Malles (Mals) to the west, and Bressanone (Brixen) and Vipiteno (Sterzing) to the northwest. Other castles were erected in strategic strongholds, such as at the mouths of tributary valleys, or atop lofty crags, themselves formidable defensive structures. Many of the forts stand in ruins, either razed after hard-fought sieges, or swept away by avalanches and landslides. A few have survived intact, and have been restored to their former glory.

The best known of these castles is surely the Castello del Buon Consiglio, in Trent, an immense building that for centuries was the residence of the bishop-princes, and is now a museum.

Also worthy of mention is the Castel Tirolo, a few kilometres outside of Merano. This remarkable monument – at once invulnerable fortress and sumptuous residence – was the home and stronghold of Mainardo II, the count of Tyrol who won that region's independence.

Famed for its 14th-century frescoes is the Castello di Avio; its long, crenelated curtain walls loom over the road that runs up to Trent.

There are many other monuments of lesser fame, an intrinsic part of the picturesque landscape. One such is the Castel Toblino, built on a spit of land extending out into the lake of Toblino; another is the Castello di Mezzocorona, stoutly built into a sheer rock cliff, or the Castello di Salorno, jutting solitary atop a lofty crag, or the Castel Presule, set on a gentle slope, or the Castello di San Martino in Badia, with strong towers amid green pastures... The list of castles, with their histories of deeds of valour and chivalry, could go on practically without end.

The Castello di Salorno, high atop a rocky crag (facing page).

The Castel Tirolo, a fortress and aristocratic home not far from Merano, looks down over the valley below.

Castel Toblino and the lake of the same name, with Castel Presule on the slopes – two voices in the ongoing dialogue between man and nature high in the Italian Alps.

From the Docks of Trieste to the Friulian Plains

Friuli-Venezia Giulia is the northeasternmost Italian region, a remarkable region with landscape ranging from coastal lagoons to Alpine summits, with cultural affinities with Mitteleuropa and the Balkans. This is a borderland, for better or worse: a crossroads of commercial prosperity, but also the theatre of murderous battles during World War I, cruelly divided after World War II. It is the home of a staunch people, many of whom emigrated to escape a tradition of poverty, while those who remained struggled to recover from a catastrophic earthquake in 1976. Let us consider Trieste, a great city on the Adriatic coast, with the Karst, or Carso highlands spreading away behind it, just a few miles from the border with the former Yugoslavia.

Locked away behind a narrow ring of walls during the darkest centuries of European history, Trieste opened out to the Adriatic in the 18th century, becoming one of the leading Mediterranean harbour cities; for two centuries it was the maritime outlet for the entire Austro-Hungarian empire under the Hapsburgs. Many fine monuments and traditions remain from that Golden Age of Trieste; foremost among them, however, is the strong flavour of Mitteleuropa that still dominates here, unlike anywhere else in Italy. On the Colle di San Giusto, the hill that has always been the heart of Trieste, stand a Roman theatre, the 14th-century cathedral of San Giusto, and a Castle, built between 1470 and 1630. Equally interesting are the stately Piazza Unità d'Italia, renovated in the late 19th and early 20th centuries, and the Rive, waterfront avenues lined with the office buildings of great

shipping companies. Of great historical interest is the Borgo Teresiano, or New Town, built at the turn of the 19th century to accommodate Trieste's growing merchant class, or the industrial districts, both old and new, whose shipyards and manufacturers have written great chapters in the city's history. Not far from Trieste, perched on a headland jutting out into the coastline of the gulf of Trieste, stands a princely building made of white Istrian stone, the Castello di Miramare. It was built in the mid-19th century

The Castello di Miramare, just outside of Trieste, is a sight that lingers in the memory of those who visit this capital of the territory of Giulia (preceding pages).

The "Barcolana," a traditional regatta on a wind-swept sea.

A broad aerial view of the city of Trieste, formerly the chief port of the Austro-Hungarian empire.

by the archduke Maximilian; he lived here before accepting the crown of Mexico and the tragic fate that came with it. The castle is a token of this haunted, tragic story, lonely in its vast and elegant Italian-style park. Just inland rises the Karst, or Carso, a limestone tableland which stretches away for kilometres inland; particularly lovely in autumn, when the leaves turn in a riot of colour. Beneath the Karst is a labyrinth of sinkholes, hollows, and subterranean streams, as yet only partly explored. Aside from subterranean marvels, the area around Trieste offers many delights: art-lovers may visit Muggia, a charming Venetian-style walled town; connoisseurs of fine wine may enjoy the whites of Collio, from the rolling hills near Gorizia.

Detail of the facade of the cathedral of the Friulian town of Gemona.

"Casoni" near the lagoon of Marano.

Karstic rock – cunningly shaped by nature – can assume an astounding array of forms.

To conclude this summary excursion through the region, let us take a bird's-eye view of the Adriatic coastline between the mouths of the rivers Isonzo and Tagliamento, where the lagoons of Grado and Marano extend, vast basins of brackish water teeming with wildlife and wetland growth. Along the coast are two of the upper Adriatic's most renowned resorts. The first is Lignano Sabbiadoro (literally, "golden-sand"),

built between the two World Wars, and aptly named. The second is Grado, an ancient fishing village with a well-preserved mediaeval centre, where narrow lanes ("calli") and busy little squares ("campielli") run past a major complex of early Christian buildings. Just inland from Grado is Aquileia, once a thriving Roman colony. It is said that the Gospel according to St Mark was first preached here, by St Mark and a series of martyred bishops. When persecution of Christianity ended, churches were built. Note, for example, the handsome 11th-century Romanesque basilica, with splendid mosaic decorations.

Udine is the historic capital of the region of Friuli; it nestles at the foot of an isolated morainic hill. From the summit, you can see the broad plain, dotted with villages, churches, and villas, and the curving arc of the Carnic and Julian Alps, as well as the Karst, or Carso, and Istria. In the centre of Udine extends the lovely Piazza della Libertà, surrounded by elegant Venetian-style buildings. The cathedral is an impressive Gothic structure built in the 14th century. Nearby, on the banks of the river Natisone, is Cividale del Friuli, a major ancient Roman colony, with ruins from that period and from the long years of Lombard rule in the Middle Ages. To the north, along the river Tagliamento, stand the towns of Gemona and Venzone, with notable monuments despite the earthquake 20 years ago.

43

The Hill of San Giusto in Trieste

It has been ascertained that ancient *Tergeste* (Trieste) was settled in prehistoric times, strategically astride the shortest route from the Adriatic Sea to the Danube basin and the Balkans. If *Tergeste* was convenient, it was also unfortunately exposed to the ravages of marauders and invaders. Given the constant perils to which ancient Trieste was exposed, the city remained clustered on the hilltop of the original settlement, safe within its walls. The hill was named San Giusto, after a saint believed to have been martyred here, in 303 A.D. This tiny plot of land was the stage for over a thousand years of Triestine history; the result is a remarkably dense array of monuments. The focal point of this venerable city centre is the peak of the hill of San Giusto, heart of the Roman colony and, in time, of the Christian community of the Middle Ages. Here stands the cathedral (San Giusto), built in the 14th century; it was the product of the joining of two existing buildings, the basilica of Santa Maria Assunta (11th century) and the church of San Giusto (9th-11th century), with a single grand nave. The five-aisle construction was endowed with a new facade and a magnificent, Gothic rose window; the interior still gleams with ancient mosaics, among the finest of the period. Nearby are gardens, dotted with venerable trees and ancient inscriptions and plaques; the remarkable views entranced visitors in the 19th cenyury. Also nearby are the ruins of two major buildings dating from Roman times: the forensic basilica and the Capitoline temple. In the basilica, business was conducted and justice meted out; the columned hall stretches nearly 90 metres in length, and over 23 metres in breadth. On the forum side is a

The castle high atop the Colle di San Giusto (facing page).

The facade and bell tower of the cathedral.

Aisle inside the church of San Giusto.

The "lapidary garden," a place of remarkably evocative atmosphere.

portico, which was probably once lined with shops. The Capitoline temple is misnamed, due to the long-held belief that it was once a temple dedicated to the Capitoline triad of gods: Jupiter, Juno, and Minerva. Instead, it was the propylaeum, or vestibule, of a major commemorative monument. Overlooking the broad Roman forum is the huge Castello di San Giusto, built beginning in the 15th century, upon a site that was fortified as early as prehistoric times. Ramparts and battlements are no longer patrolled by soldiers with halberds; they now offer delightful views of Trieste and the gulf; the spacious halls and courts of the castle are now used for exhibitions and outdoor performances. By all means, make the climb up to the castle, and then run your gaze along the slopes in search of other landmarks and monuments: you will see churches, palaces, and a fine Roman theatre seating 6,000, built in the 1st-2nd century. Monuments are not all the hill has to offer; you can detect the original urban layout of mediaeval Trieste, with narrow lanes and tiny little squares crammed with buildings, as touching and impressive in their way as the more glorious ruins of antiquity. 45

The Ancient Basilicas of Aquileia and Grado

Aquileia and Grado, throughout their long and eventful histories, were always close-linked counterparts: one stood inland while the other stood by the sea; one was surrounded by fertile farmland and major roads, the other stood on the shore of a great lagoon, and was the terminus of the chief sea routes of the northern Adriatic Sea.

The first of the two to prosper was Aquileia. Founded in 181 B.C. to defend the northeastern plains of Italy from from Gauls and Istrian marauders, it soon became the central market town of a vast hinterland, and a great commercial power.

With the fall of the Empire, however, it reverted to its original state: an outpost threatened by barbarian incursions and warring emperors.

The Romanesque basilica of Aquileia possesses notable works of art (facing page).

The Roman Forum of Aquileia, a witness to ancient splendour.

The interior, with the magnificent ambo, and the exterior of the Basilica di Sant'Eufemia, at Grado.

Devastated by Attila in 452 A.D., Aquileia's inhabitants fled, and many took refuge in Grado. This lagoon city was protected by its natural isolation; in time it grew, and became a major rival of its neighbour, Aquileia. Around the year 1000, Aquileia recovered its position as the crossroads of trade with Germany, but just a few centuries later malaria devastated its populace, causing a decline that finally sealed its fate. Grado suffered roughly the same destiny, throttled by Venetian domination. Each town dwindled, cut off from the mainstream of history: a particularly ironic twist considering the array of impressive monuments each boasts, worthy of the mightiest capitals. Particularly noteworthy are the Roman ruins of Aquileia, including the riverside harbour and the forum; even more impressive are the relics of mediaeval Christianity. Foremost among them is the mighty basilica, with its free-standing campanile, rebuilt in the Romanesque style from 1021 to 1031; it stands atop ancient places of worship dating from the 4th century. Inside, the nave and two aisles feature the largest mosaic floor found in western Christendom; intact, lovely, and dating from the earliest structure.

Eleventh-century frescoes adorn both apse and crypt, while the left aisle features the Chapel of the Holy Sepulchre, a remarkable structure with a circular plan.

Equally remarkable are the early Christian buildings of Grado. The Basilica di Sant'Eufemia, to name only the largest, dates from the 6th century, and is built of reused Roman materials on the site of an earlier church. Inside, the two aisles are separated from the nave with Roman columns; note the very fine mosaic floor. Also worthy of note is the ambo, assembled from materials spanning a millennium of history. These are two of mediaeval Italy's greatest basilicas: a splendid creation of human skill and labour.

The Exquisite Colours of Giambattista Tiepolo's Work in Udine

Three centuries ago, in 1696, the great Italian decorative painter Giambattista Tiepolo was born in Venice. This greatest and most quintessentially rococo figure of his age was an unrivalled creator of commemorative frescoes. Tiepolo's compositions are full of movement and energy, and a sense of awe is created by the use of dramatically exaggerated foreshortening and subtle chiaroscuro. As spectacular as they are improbable, these ethereal scenes, with Tiepolo's characteristically light touch and sense of real atmosphere, seem almost

in the adjoining Sala del Tribunale, or courtroom, reveal a precocious mastery of form and colour and a skill at creating dazzling effects of lighting that awoke great admiration. This great project made Tiepolo's reputation; thenceforth he was showered with commissions in Italy and throughout Europe; he worked in Milan, Bergamo, Vicenza, Venice, and then in Germany and Spain. Rather than retracing Tiepolo's footsteps across the continent, however, let us enjoy the other works this great artist left in Udine. We should begin in the Duomo, or cathedral; here,

monumental heart of this Friulian capital. You will pass through an archway designed by Andrea Palladio in 1556, to reach Piazza della Libertà, the very heart of Udine, lined by an elegant complex of buildings in the Venetian style. On one side of the square stands the Loggia del Lionello or Palazzo del Comune, Udine's town hall, an exquisite example of a loggiaed Gothic palazzo; facing it is the Porticato di San Giovanni, a showy Renaissance portico topped by a soaring clock tower. At the centre of the square is a Renaissance fountain, by Giovanni da Carrara.

excuses to unleash a vivid imagination. Any traveller wishing to trace Tiepolo's progress by retracing the early steps of his career should begin in Venice, where the aristocratic Dolfin family gave him his first major assignment when he was still in his early twenties. Shortly thereafter, Dionisio, the archbishop of Udine, and a Dolfin, commissioned Tiepolo to decorate a number of rooms in the Archbishop's Palace. The modern traveller may thus travel to this Friulian capital to admire Tiepolo's first masterpiece. The Bible scenes in the gallery and the renowned *Judgment of Solomon*

note the outstanding frescoes in the Chapel of the Sacrament, done in the same period, as well as a few panels from Tiepolo's later years. The adjacent Oratorio della Purità features a superb ceiling fresco of the Assumption, as well as an altarpiece. The last step in retracing Tiepolo's stay in Udine is the Castello, a vast 16th-century castle designed by Giovanni da Udine and Giovanni Fontana, and more palace than fortress. It now houses the Civic Museum; an entire hall is devoted to work by Tiepolo.

That covers Tiepolo's bequest to Udine, but you should certainly tour the

A comfortable rest, and then we must be off, in search of the next Tiepolo masterpiece, in quest of new examples of the magical colour and light created by this Venetian master of the rococo.

The Porticato di San Giovanni, beneath the 16th-century clock tower, is the central feature of the monumental complex of the Friulian capital of Udine, in Piazza della Libertà (facing page).

Frescoes of Bible stories by Giambattista Tiepolo in the Archbishop's Palace; clearly the painter enjoyed a prosperous and successful stay in Udine.

The Lombard Heritage of Cividale del Friuli

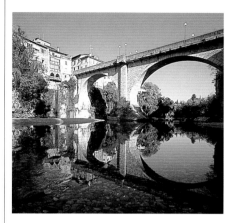

Not far from Udine, rising high above the banks of the river Natisone, stands Cividale del Friuli. Built on the site of a garrison established by Caesar to protect the hinterland of the port system of Aquileia and Grado, Cividale was occupied by the Lombards in 568 A.D., becoming the capital of their first Italian duchy. By the 8th century, Cividale was a thriving town, the birthplace of two kings – Ratchis and Astolfo – as well as of the historian and poet Paulus Diaconus, or Paul the Deacon, and the patriarch St Paulinus, poet, theologian, and counsellor to Charlemagne, first Holy Roman Emperor, and the conqueror of the Lombards.

Cividale still preserves a compact urban layout and a nearly intact circle of walls, which date from its golden age;

Detail of the interior of the Tempietto Longobardo (facing page).

The Ponte del Diavolo over the river Natisone.

Art attains heights of exquisite expression in the Tempietto Longobardo.

A Lombard buckle, part of the trove of objects found in the Museums of Cividale.

the walls were rebuilt in the Middle Ages. The Duomo, Cividale's cathedral, stands in a broad square in the heart of town; this solemn Renaissance church is one of the prime attractions in this tour of the land of the ancient Lombards. Nearby is the Christian Museum, with masterpieces of sculpture and the goldsmith's craft. Particularly renowned are: an octagonal shrine from the 8th-century baptistery of San Callisto; the altar of Ratchis, also from the 8th century; and a marble throne dating from the 9th century, though possibly assembled from older sections. Of special note are the antiquities on display in the nearby Archeological Museum: note a Roman sarcophagus, and the treasure of Duke Gisulfo (goldsmithery and weapons). In the vicinity is the Celtic Hypogaeum, an underground complex dating from the 5th century; later used as a prison by the Lombards. The lofty central chamber, hewn out of living rock, branches off into a series of subterranean passages leading down

to the river. The most extraordinary relic of the Lombard presence in Cividale is the Tempietto, an ancient Lombard chapel, set in the Borgo Brossana, a quarter near the earliest town centre. Legend has it that Piltrude, a Lombard queen, had it built; scholars prefer to date it to the 8th-9th centuries. This square structure is covered by a high cross vault; an iconostasis screens off the apsidal area, with three low barrel vaults supported by two rows of columns. The abundance of reused Roman and Byzantine materials, the large frescoes and exquisite old stuccoes, all dating from the original construction, give this monument its remarkable charm. This singular example of the art of the High Middle Ages provides a fitting conclusion.

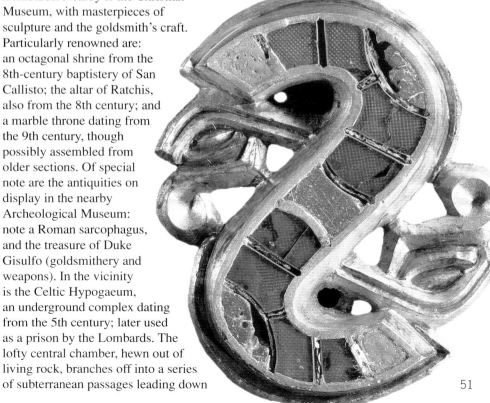

Landscapes of the Po Valley, Amid Waterways and Countryside

There was a time when the Alps were blanketed with perennial snows. Glaciers, more immense than our wildest imaginings, carved out valleys with their slow progress, and then oozed out over the plains like a chilly flow of lava. As they melted, giant torrents of water rushed down to the sea. Once the glaciers were gone and the floods had subsided, mammoths, cave bears, and troglodytes

emerged onto the face of the land. These were the violent birth pangs of the lovely Italian peninsula; this is how Italy acquired the appearance that is still praised so lavishly. To understand this, let us follow the flight of a migratory bird as it wings over the Brenner Pass

The river Oglio flows slowly and silently among the trees (preceding pages).

The towers of Garisenda and Asinelli in Bologna.

Piazza Grande and the cathedral of Modena.

The Po Valley, where hard work has hemmed in the land with geometric boundaries.

and drops down to the silvery waters of Lake Garda. The only hint of that remote glacial turmoil is offered by the steep coastline of the lake; the climate is mild, and the vegetation is distinctly Mediterranean. That humans soon noticed the beauty of this lake is evident from the history of lakeside cities of long and noble pedigree, such as Verona, or from the poetry of Catullus. *Odi et amo*, Catullus wrote. It is said that this passionate lyric poet lived in the 1st century B.C. in the great villa

located at the point of the peninsula of Sirmione. Let us then move further south, along the river Mincio, which flows out of the lake and cuts through the amphitheatre of hills that mark the southernmost expansion of the giant ancient glacier. What the mighty glacier plowed up were sterile mounds; the passage of thousands of years and the work of industrious farmers and architects have made them verdant hillsides, covered with vacation houses and ripening grapevines. The Mincio then spreads out, forming the three

lakes that gird Mantua. Long ago this was the capital of the Gonzaga, and the finest artists of the Renaissance were summoned here. Just a bit further downstream, the Mincio flows into the Po, Italy's largest river, the sire and lord of its valley plain. The Po flows east to the Adriatic, and marks almost the entire length of the boundary between Lombardy, Veneto, and Emilia. High embankments, from which geometric rows of poplar trees run away as far as the eye can see, divide the Po from the fields planted in corn and sunflowers. On every side extend fertile farmlands, crisscrossed by canals named after this or that "gran signore" who paid for their excavation. Here is a green and seemingly endless horizon, broken only by large farmhouses and the narrow bell towers of the occasional village. Motionless under the bright sunshine, amidst the monotonous chirping of crickets, a silence broken only by the mechanical back-and-forth of tractors and the spraying jets of water arcing out over the fields. Here, the bird's-eye view of our feathered migrator – following the course of the Po – ranges from south to east, from the plains around Bologna, hemmed in by the first Apennine foothills, all the way to the fields around Ferrara, which fade

into the brackish wetlands of the great delta and the blue of the Adriatic Sea. In one direction is an increasingly crowded landscape, on the other is the secluded world of the major reclamation projects, the last coastal lagoons and wetlands, "sanctuaries" of nature. The southern section of the Po valley is crossed by the Via Emilia which runs straight from Piacenza to Rimini, passing through Parma, Reggio Emilia, Modena, Bologna, and Forlì. Drive along this highway, and you are driving through

20 long centuries of history, despite the modern structures of one of Italy's richest and most productive agricultural and industrial areas. At a greater elevation, running through the tortuous landscape of Apennine badlands and clay fields, is the Via dei Castelli, or Road of Castles, linking fortified towns and isolated strongholds, crossing at the valley floors the roads running up to the Apennine passes leading south to Liguria and Tuscany. Along the roads running northeast to Venice stand the cities of Ferrara, inland, and Ravenna, practically on the coast. This completes the tour of provincial capitals of Emilia-Romagna. A series of cities linked one to another and to the great dynasties of Europe through the intricate interplay of history; an "art gallery" capable of satisfying the most demanding connoisseurs on earth. Every era is represented here: the great buildings of the late Roman Empire and the mosaics and churches of early Christianity; the majestic Romanesque forms of medieval cathedrals and baptisteries; the sumptuous palazzi of the Renaissance; and the modern era, with all that that entails. Let us close with a thumbnail portrait of Bologna, known as "La Dotta," or The Learned One, with its spectacular Piazza Maggiore, its two leaning towers, and Europe's oldest university. Midway between the beach resorts of the lively Romagna Riviera and small-town Italy, linked to Europe by long-term cultural affinities, but far from the wretched excess of certain major cities, Bologna is a noblewoman, at its ease in learned drawing-room conversation, as well as in the kitchen, preparing the food for which it is famous worldwide.

A view of the Arena of Verona.

Mantua, ancient Lombard city, founded where the river Mincio quietly flows, just before it pours into the mighty river Po.

The western shore of Lake Garda.

A Haven of Poetry Amid the Olive Groves of Lake Garda

Sirmione greets the traveller with the lovely, but chastening, sight of the fortress that the Della Scala family built in the 13th century. This massive fortification, with crenelated towers and walls, surrounded on all sides by water, is remarkably intact and architecturally quite impressive. It is perhaps just a touch daunting, considering the languid atmosphere described by writers. Lake Garda is a gentle, relaxing place; it knits up the raveled sleeve of care. Perhaps that is why it was so dear to the troubled heart of the Roman lyric poet Catullus. Catullus was able to convert his emotional pain into high poetry; he was a charming apologist of love for love's sake. Born in Verona, he had inherited two villas, one near Rome, the other here in Sirmione. In the villa near Rome, Catullus probably lived through the most ecstatic moments of his love affair with a lovely and unscrupulous married woman, whom he disguised in his verses with the name of "Lesbia"; he retired to the villa in Sirmione, on the other hand, to try to forget his lover, no more faithful to him than she had been to her husband. We know of this unhappy affair and the subsequent retreat to Sirmione from Catullus's own poetry; in the 16th century one enthusiastic poetry-lover decided that the impressive ruins on the peninsula of Sirmione were doubtless the poet's villa. The vast foundations, which resemble caverns, led to the doubly erroneous name of "Grotto of Catullus"; modern archeologists, on the other hand, assure us that this was a villa from the time of the Empire, and therefore as much as two centuries after Catullus's death. Still, there are some fragments of the villa that date from the 1st century B.C., and therefore it is just possible that

the first inhabitant was the star-crossed poet. The very flimsiness of the possibility is itself poetic.

Let us return to the "Grotto." Consider the size of this huge, rectangular building: 230 x 105 metres, high on a rocky spur extending into the lake. A monumental entrance leads to the interior: huge halls for entertaining, hot baths, pools, and the living quarters, arrayed around a large central courtyard, with a vast terrace overlooking the lake. The whole place, of course, was sumptuously decorated, as we can see from the remaining paintings and stuccoes. The luxury becomes even more sybaritic if we are ever able to be sure that the lordly baths enjoyed in this villa made use of the hot springs – not only hot,

Lake Garda and Salò from the ruins of the so-called villa of Catullus (facing page).

The harmony of nature has encouraged humans to create elegant architecture here.

The Rocca Scaligera now stands in peace.

but rich in minerals and slightly radioactive – that flow from the lake bottom, and are nowadays used for their curative properties. If this detail is ever determined with certainty, it will certainly add to the allure of this remarkable villa.

The Idle Pleasures of the Gonzaga of Mantua

In 1328, the long reign of the Gonzaga began in Mantua. These enlightened princes would strive for nearly four centuries to surround themselves with brilliant minds and to embellish their city. The height of their artistic fervor and patronage of the arts came with the arrival of Isabella d'Este (1474-1539), the learned wife of Francesco II; she commissioned works from Leonardo da Vinci and Giovanni Bellini, and greeted Giulio Romano – the talented pupil of Raphael – in 1524, when he arrived in Mantua, fresh from his triumphs in Rome. Federico II, Isabella's son, gave Giulio *carte blanche* to construct and decorate all the buildings required to make Mantua and its countryside one large work of art. And, indeed, under the supervision of Giulio Romano, Mantua was largely rebuilt; work was also done to stem the frequent floods of the river Mincio. Giulio's greatest creation, however, was the Palazzo Te, a pleasure house built for entertainment and banqueting, with loggias, gardens, and grottoes. It was one of the wonders of its time, entirely designed and built by Giulio Romano and his various assistants and students. This building, erected on the site of the old Gonzaga stables, stood on an island; its low profile and the rustic treatment of the facade perfectly accorded with the surrounding gardens and streams. Comprising four low buildings enclosing a courtyard, the Palazzo – recently restored – contains many rooms, lavishly decorated with grotesques and frescoes that exalt the power of love and military glory.

In particular, you should note the Sala di Psiche, with a series of frescoes of the myth of Cupid and Psyche – as told by Apuleius, a late Roman author – in one of the best known works of Italian Mannerism. Also, note the unforgettable Sala dei Giganti, hailed by Vasari and many other critics for the power and fascination it exerts on the viewer; the ceiling and walls are decorated with one continuous depiction of the destruction of the Giants, struck by Jupiter's thunderbolts and overwhelmed by the collapse of Olympus, which they were trying to scale.

The frescoes by Giulio Romano in the Sala dei Giganti (facing page).

The exedra of the gardens and the succession of scenes that greet the visitor to Palazzo Te.

In the Sala di Psiche, masterpieces of Italian Mannerist painting.

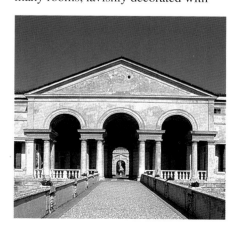

The Po Delta, an Ever-Changing World of Water

Many years ago, before rivers and streams were shaped and hemmed in by embankments and irrigation projects, a great river would run down to the sea through a gradual and shifting territory, a territory that was intensely affected by the course of the waters. This was the delta.

Rivers still flow free on the "front line" where the sands of the riverbed continually dig new trenches. In the "side-show" however, things are different. Here, for centuries, man has been quick to see opportunities for profit. Here, a river has truly become a manmade thing; a giant construction that covers not only the delta and all its watercourses, but even the adjoining coastline and meadowlands. This is the case with the delta of the great river Po. This enormous territory is a vast and intricate mosaic of environments, ranging from the lagoon of Chioggia to the pine woods of Ravenna: inland marshes, coastal salt-water ponds, great embankments for the breeding of fish, reedbeds, canals, beaches, dunes, salt-flats, and ancient groves and woods amidst the meadowlands – these are all facets of a natural heritage that we have learned to value, a heritage that is now protected by a series of natural parks and preserves. For anyone who drives along the busy Via Romea, it is difficult to imagine that, hidden in the nearby landscape, there could be settings of such primeval beauty, untouched and intact. There are great colonies of herons and cormorants, migrating flocks of ducks, such rare sightings as stags or spoonbills. Equally unexpected are the remarkable works of art and bits of history that seem to surface at every bend in the river. Consider, for instance, the Castello della Mesola, a hunting lodge that once belonged to the Este

family, surrounded by an immense estate – the Boscone – which is actually a small patch of the great and primordial forest that once covered the entire Po valley.

Or consider the Abbey of Pomposa, founded by Benedictine monks.
The tall bell tower still juts up from the monotonous line of reclaimed land, to hint at what solitary places these once were. The abbey was a way-station for pilgrims on their way to Rome and it is

still a treasure chest of religious art. We however, are heading north, toward Chioggia, and that remarkable town still has the appearance of an ancient fishing village, at least in the historical centre. The street names – "calli" and "fondamenta" – reflect the same lilting dialect found throughout the lagoon, and especially in the Queen of the Lagoon – Venice. We continue through this landscape of reclaimed farmland, immersed in silence and stillness. The atmosphere is unique, here, and we soon encounter an old acquaintance, and the real protagonist of this last stretch of plain: the river Po, running shallow through widespread expanses of gravel and sand, dotted here and there by great silvery stands of willows and the tufts of pioneer grasses that invade after every flood of the river.

A little egret admires its reflection in the waters that flow to the Adriatic Sea (facing page).

Moorage and waterways at Scardovari and in the Polesine: those who work in the Po delta know both the calm and the pent-up wrath of the great father of Italian rivers.

Oyster farming – here land and water mix and merge.

Ferrara and the Luxuries of the Renaissance

Ferrara was founded in the high Middle Ages; it prospered and expanded after the year 1000 as a market place and river port on the Po. A decisive factor in Ferrara's history was the emergence of the House of Este in the 13th century. This dynasty ruled Ferrara over the next three centuries, guiding the city's growth through three successive "additions." By additions, they meant the wholesale construction of new quarters of town. These additions however were cunning creations; they meshed perfectly with the old town, and immediately became functioning parts of a new and larger Ferrara.

The Castello Estense stands overlooking the Renaissance "addition" (facing page).

The facade of the Palazzo dei Diamanti.

A detail of the non-religious frescoes that decorate Palazzo Schifanoia.

Maze in the garden of Palazzo Costabili.

The most important of these additions was created in the Renaissance by Ercole d'Este, under the supervision of his architect, the great Biagio Rossetti. The salient features of the new northern quarter were the two main thoroughfares, intersecting at right angles; along this grid every detail – every palazzo, church, or monument – should be considered not on its own merits, but as part of the whole.

In particular, Corso Ercole d'Este, the avenue running north from the Castello Estense, was originally meant as a sort of private road, serving the homes of the duke's family and friends. In this sense, it lies at the heart of one of the most significant and aristocratic urban settings in all Italy.

The most important feature of Corso Ercole d'Este is the Palazzo dei Diamanti, set at the intersection with the other main avenue in the "Herculean Addition." This palazzo is one of the architectural masterpieces of the Italian Renaissance. It is faced with 8,500 diamond-shaped ashlars, creating a remarkable effect, as if the building were clad in a glittering suit of armour. The palazzo was the residence of the Este family until Ferrara came under the rule of the Papal state; now it houses art exhibitions. Upstairs is the Pinacoteca Nazionale, an art gallery with a fine collection of paintings from Ferrara's golden age. From here, Corso Ercole d'Este runs past a series of aristocratic palazzi to the town walls. Here was once the Porta degli Angeli, one of the town gates. It was sealed up in 1598 after Cesare d'Este, the last duke of Ferrara, left for the last time.

Everyday Life Flows By Under the Porticoes of Bologna

The ancient city grid of Bologna is distinctive and clearly legible: it resembles a tree, its trunk being the main street of the original Roman colony – a trunk that then coincides with the Via Emilia – with branches that spread out from the central fulcrum of the two leaning towers. The various mediaeval avenues spread out from there, radiating toward the outskirts of town. This organizational structure developed gradually into its modern-day form sometime after the year 1000, when the thriving city and the newly founded university employed

many builders and architects. Since the area within the earliest walls was soon packed and crowded – an area marked by the numerous towers belonging to noble families – a second ring of walls was begun, being quickly completed by 1192. Even this new territory was immediately occupied, in so chaotic and frenzied an expansion that the city was forced to act. Urban regulations were passed: it was forbidden to build streets with less than a minimum width; and, most important, it became a legal requirement to build porticoes along every new road. Soon Bologna began to acquire the porticoes that are now so much a part of its appearance. In the late 13th century, this town was one of the ten largest in Europe, with a population of 50,000. Still, Bologna needed even more room to grow: at this point outside the walls.
A third ring of walls was completed in 1374, enclosing a total area of 420 hectares, making Bologna one of the largest cities in Italy in terms of surface area; this space is what is now called the historical centre. The triumphant development of the porticoes of

Bologna, nonetheless, was far from done. Over the ensuing centuries, despite various economic crises, political turmoil, and plagues, a great project of urban embellishment was carried on. Roads were straightened, new squares were hewn out, the main roads leading into the centre of town were beautified – just so many new opportunities to build new porticoes. And these porticoes are highly democratic structures, as we can still see. They cover and protect workshop, store, and palazzo; tenured professor and the struggling student.

A broad view of the centre of Bologna, showing its urban grid (facing page).

A long line of columns and pillars leads up to the church of the Madonna di San Luca.

The interplay of light and shadow beneath the porticoes.

The streets of Bologna abound in facades; note the church of Santo Stefano.

Along the Ligurian Rivieras

Along the Lovely and Hard-Working Ligurian Rivieras

An arc of mountains high over the sea; narrow valleys criss-crossed by mountain streambeds, sometimes dry and sometimes filled with thunderous torrents; slopes that plunge down, the heights clad in chestnut groves and nearer the sea, Mediterranean maquis; a series of cities, wedged into the narrow plains, and coastal villages, perched on steep slopes and promontories; a forgotten archipelago of mountain villages; a welter of roads and railroads; a mosaic of vegetable gardens, greenhouses, and orchards; crowded busy ports and factories; a blend of architecture, ranging from the spontaneous to the classical to beachfront holiday homes. Liguria is profoundly linked to the sea; it is a region devoted to trading; in some ways it is English in its understated skepticism. This is Liguria as seen from above, stretching in a broad arc that

encompasses a sea that is more than just a view or a horizon; this water, to the Ligurians, is farmland and highway. The centre of the region is the great city of Genoa, the offspring of the slightly profit-oriented and decidedly piratesque ambitions of the Crusades; the Crusades made Genoa a major maritime power. That power and wealth can still be detected in the magnificence of the city itself; it now results in an expanding

network of suburbs. Luckily, it is easy to escape this "endless megalopolis" – weigh anchor and "coast" along the shoreline toward lovelier places. You do not actually need to set sail; it is quite enough to follow the Via Aurelia, a road that runs along the coast; or you can take a train or the autostrada, higher up along the coast. Head west and you will soon reach Savona, outlet to the sea for a mountainous region whose valleys are traditionally trade routes inland to Piedmont. Your next port of call may be the ancient town of Noli, with its nearly intact walls. Then you will sail past Finale Ligure, with its lovely hinterland. Another notable sight in this tour of the Riviera di Ponente (or Western Riviera) is Albenga, at the base of the montainous triangle that extends toward the French border. Then come the white sand beaches of Alassio, a charming town that attracted great flocks of migrating Britons in the 19th century. And then, as if to end a chapter, comes the handsome coastline of Laigueglia and the built-up plain of Andora. Let us turn the page: now we encounter a series of valleys running gently down to the sea. Along the coast, you should note Cervo, a mediaeval village perched high atop a rocky spur; Imperia, capital with a split personality, born of the fusion of Porto Maurizio, the outlet for a vast inland territory of wooded hills, and Oneglia, the centre of a fruited plain along the river Impero. With the

The marina of Camogli at sunset (preceding pages).

Genoa, an ancient maritime Republic and a modern, thriving city.

An old watchtower in the Finalese region.

Valle Argentina, which you reach next, Liguria turns its attention inland again, passing from the Mediterranean environment of the mediaeval Taggia, to unexpected Alpine prospects. Next is the amphitheatre of San Remo, set in an ideal location between two ridges that shelter it from wind; palm trees grow here, and there is a local industry based on growing carnations. Extending seaward is Bordighera with its double soul: the historical centre, above Capo Sant'Ampelio,

and the modern section, on the plain, still a garden district. As far west as you can go is the Roia valley; across the French border, it climbs up to the Col du Tende; from there a road leads down into Piedmont. At the border itself is Ventimiglia, and it conceals one last jewel of the Italian Riviera: the promontory of La Mortola, with the exotic gardens of Villa Hanbury. Equally intriguing is the Riviera di Levante (or Eastern Riviera), which extends eastward from Genoa.

You will soon reach the promontory of Portofino, a port in any storm. Before it extends the Golfo Paradiso, overlooked by Camogli, an ancient fishing village which has somehow survived the flood tide of tourists and maintained its charm. Like so many gems set in the verdant spur are San Fruttuoso, a tiny fishing village clustered around an historic abbey, and Portofino itself, an ancient port town that is now a tourist attraction for the rich and famous.

On the Golfo del Tigullio, to the east, are Santa Margherita and Rapallo, in a lovely and strategic setting. A new air can be felt blowing down from the valleys that radiate out from Chiavari, an air with the smell of the Po valley – air of Piacenza or Parma, depending on which Apennine pass it blows over. The same is true of Sestri Levante, which establishes a first link with Tuscany, over the Val di Vara. As you continue along, the coast becomes more jagged and the roads move inland, to the wooded crags of the Bracco; this shift in landscape foreshadows the wild beauty of the Cinque Terre. This nature is harsh, but fascinating, and it becomes tame again only at Portovenere, alluring name of an alluring port, where a rocky ridge plunges down into the sea. The town winds along, a single line of housefronts, with two mediaeval churches and a more recent castle. Facing it is the promontory of Montemarcello, with the mediaeval town of Lerici, beneath its high castle. Further along the inlet is La Spezia, an old town and a major naval base. The end of the Levante is Tuscan: this is the mouth of the river Magra, largely running through Tuscany. This frontier land features the ruins of Luni, an ancient Roman port, and Sarzana, a longtime guardian of the road that runs from the pass of the Cisa down to the Tyrrhenian Sea.

Sestri Levante, which marks the eastern boundary of the Golfo del Tigullio, is a renowned tourist attraction and a trading centre with a long history.

Flowers in the Riviera: The mild climate has helped over the course of the centuries to enhance the allure of this land between mountains and sea.

The towers of the fortress of Sarzanello, built in 1322 by Castruccio Castracani.

Listening to the Ancient Voices of Albenga

It is not an everyday experience to walk into a setting out of the Middle Ages, and to gaze across a square that was once the centre of an ancient Roman municipium. It may be a moving experience, as you stand before the baptistery, to consider that this building was erected in early Christian times, that it survived the raids of barbarians and Saracens, and that it even outlived its cathedral, which the citizens of Albenga did not rebuild for several centuries. The new cathedral stands on the site of the old one, however, and is the same size, and has an exceedingly handsome bell tower. It is equally moving, as you stand before the 14th-century Palazzo Vecchio with its tall tower, to think of the travails of a city struggling for supremacy in trade, and in some cases, for its very liberty. And it is pleasant to cast your mind back to the atmosphere of bygone days, wandering footloose as you listen to the voices of secluded corners: like those in the little square behind the cathedral, where three lions carved from peperino and a tall tower speak of the pride of the patrician family that lived there; or the voices that emanate from the collections of the town museums, grouped around the square, voices of the ancient Italic tribes, of the wreck of an ancient Roman cargo ship, of centuries of stalwart faith; or the voices that filter

out of the atriums of palazzi, bedecked with ancient epigraphs and stones; or the voices that can be heard in old shops, or conversations of passers-by. All these voices are heard in Albenga, which – as the encyclopaedia tells us – was an ancient capital of the Ingauni

Ligurians (*Albium Ingaunum*), then a Roman municipium and episcopal see, destroyed more than once during the Dark Ages but rebuilt after the year 1000, one of the first of the maritime city-states to gain its independence.

Once Albenga lost its ancient commercial importance, the encyclopaedias conclude, it devoted itself to agriculture and is now renowned for its hothouse produce. Particularly fine is its delectabe asparagus.

The bell tower of the cathedral and the towers overlooking Piazza San Michele (facing page).

The exterior of a window in the baptistery.

A distinctive view of the mediaeval centre.

The loggia of the Palazzo Vecchio.

Portofino, From Fishing Village to Exclusive Resort

The ancient harbour of *Portus Delphini* dates back into the mists of time; its venerable age must be attributed to its ideal location, a perfect haven for vessels coasting along the Ligurian shore. The port town's original centre lay near the church of San Martino; in time, Portofino expanded inland and along the waterfront. Under Genoan rule, it became what we see today, with a main piazza overlooking the slipway, where smaller vessels were hauled up for scraping and repairs, and the two larger quays, where freighters once

changed much physically over the past century, and the houses have the same facades, painted the same colours, much has changed within. In the space of a few generations, the great-grandchildren of fishermen, sailors, and shipwrights have become hotel-owners and travel agents. The old houses of the little port town are now home to the rich and famous. The waters of the bay are now tossed by the wakes of expensive speedboats; the only sails in sight belong to expensive vintage yachts, and the old storage areas now

loaded and unloaded their goods. Lining the marina is a compact row of houses, some as tall as six stories; every so often, a narrow stairway runs uphill between them. This architecture is traditional in Ligurian port towns, and forms part of Portofino's defenses: defenses that were often useful, what with the frequent raids by Saracen pirates and attacks by the long-time enemy, Pisa. The ground floor was set aside for storing merchandise and marine supplies; the upper floors were the living quarters, largely inhabited by local fishermen or by mariners working on coasting vessels.

At anchor, further out, were the "leudi," the capacious local vessels used to carry foodstuffs. The "leudi" provided a vital lifeline with the other little villages along the coastline, which were rarely served by road. Inland, behind the little town, rise the green slopes of the promontory, dotted with Mediterranean underbrush, or maquis, and stands of oak and chestnut trees, extending along the gulleys and slopes; the trees favour the higher ground, the underbrush extends down to the seashore. All of this evokes the human context and the natural setting of Portofino; although it has not

glitter with lavish shop windows. Just take a step back, however, as if you were admiring a great painting, and the details lose their sharpness, while the setting as a whole regains its remarkable charm.

The warm and enchanting hues of the houses of Portofino (facing page).

From the square that stands before the church of San Giorgio you can enjoy a fine view of the town below.

The marina, an attraction for prosperous tourists.

Cinque Terre, Five Lands Lost in Time

The Cinque Terre (Five Lands) – Riomaggiore, Manarola, Corniglia, Vernazza, and Monterosso – are five villages, linked by a stretch of unrivalled seashore, where the high rocky coastline plunges down to the sea in a succession of coves and shoals bordered by the iridescent green of the Mediterranean maquis; yellow sprays of broom and scattered pine trees take

root in inaccessible niches and nooks. Most breathtaking of all is the sight of terraced farmland: the coastline is festooned with them, vineyards, olive groves, fruit orchards, stretching from the water's edge all the way up to the line of trees that crowns the hilltops.

It is natural to wonder just what prompted human beings to undertake this mammoth task, to cut away rock and mountain slope, terracing foot by foot. Fair enough, fine wines have been made here for centuries. Dante, Petrarch, and Boccaccio have all sung their praises, but it still does not explain the backbreaking labour involved. Perhaps, in olden times, when neither

land nor sea afforded safety, these dizzyingly steep cliffs seemed to offer refuge, tempting settlers to force their way up them. Centuries of sweat and blood changed the landscape, though it remains lovely. Where the landscape is too harsh for vineyards and vegetable gardens, the lush Mediterranean maquis provides a harmonious counterpoint. The five villages are themselves monuments to the stubborn industry of the Ligurians, and are unequalled in their rugged beauty. Riomaggiore, Manarola, and Vernazza stand at the bottom of narrow valleys facing the sea, houses clustered along the steep slopes in a compact front, broken only by narrow and precipitous stairways, a barrier against sea-borne raiders. Corniglia stands high atop a promontory, rising sheer from the

sea, a farming town with renowned vineyards, overlooking a broad hollow. Monterosso is a fishing village on a wide inlet; Genoa provided the town with fortifications and watchtowers against pirate raids and attacks by the rival city of Pisa.

The Cinque Terre, five villages, long isolated, that have preserved beauty and tradition that leave all visitors astonished.

The steep coasts of Riomaggiore, with the renowned Via dell'Amore – Street of Love (facing page).

The broad bay of Monterosso.

Manarola, standing high on a cliff.

The marina of Vernazza.

Corniglia, a jewel set in the mountainside.

75

Portovenere, the Port of Venus Embraces the Sea

Venus, as we all know, was born from the spray and foam of the sea. Botticelli, in his renowned *Birth of Venus*, depicted the new-born goddess being driven shoreward by the gentle breath of Zephyr, to the greeting of Flora, the Roman goddess of flowers. And Portovenere (literally, "Port Venus") might seem somewhat boastful in its name, as if this were a town that could offer a goddess a fitting welcome.

The deity of beauty and love would hardly be disappointed to land here, however. An exquisite setting, at the tip of a promontory jutting out into the sea; a mild climate; a gulf of the sea sheltered from storms and waves. It was not Venus, but the Genoan fleet that landed here in 1113; the objectives were quite prosaic: Portovenere was just one more outpost in Genoa's conquest of the Riviera di Levante. The Genoans built a naval base here, and every building, from forts to homes to churches, was built to withstand attack and siege.

The winding road at the base of the promontory, therefore, was lined with a compact row of houses. The facade of each house was narrow; the house itself extended back quite a way; and the number of floors decreasing with the angle of the slope. Narrow passages linked the waterfront with the uphill

section of town; they could be easily defended against enemy attack. This is the renowned "Calata Doria," the multicoloured "palazzata a mare," or waterfront, one of the loveliest sights in Portovenere.

Rivalling it in picturesque charm is the sight of the Gothic church of San Pietro, standing alone at the tip of the promontory, the traditional destination of a romantic stroll through Portovenere. Do not overlook the equally entrancing walk up to the high part of town, leading past the collegiate church of San Lorenzo, originally Romanesque, but with Gothic and Renaissance additions, and then up to the castle. First built in 1162, then rebuilt in the 16th and 17th centuries, the castle is an impressive piece of military architecture, with a fine vista of the gulf of La Spezia and the open sea.

Doubtless, however, the most memorable view of Portovenere is the harbour itself, at the fall of night, when a soft breeze springs up. The voices die down, and over the "calata" the dying light of sunset gives way to the glitter of the earliest

stars. It is pleasant to stroll along the waterfront, peering through the darkness at the black silhouettes of islands and promontory, seeing new shapes and colours under the bright streetlamps, to hear voices leaking through the closed shutters, imagining the people hidden behind them. An intriguing, slightly intrusive way of passing the time, when darkness erases the outlines of reality, and one can take flights of fancy into the past.

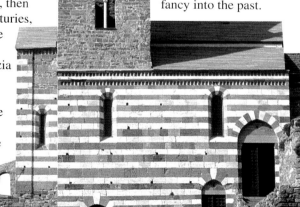

The tip of the promontory of Portovenere in the light of sunset (facing page).

Bits of coastline seen from the loggia that flanks the church of San Pietro.

The multicoloured Calata Doria, beneath the collegiate church of San Lorenzo and the castle.

The distinctive Gothic church of San Pietro.

Following the Pilgrim Roads of Tuscany

The visitor who wishes to explore the infinitely varied world of Tuscan art and architecture should beware the dangers of "art-lover's syndrome" – a sense of vertigo and confusion in the face of such splendour. The safest way to proceed is to cleave to a theme, thus narrowing the focus to a more accessible body of work. Having accepted this principle, the truly European traveller may choose to follow the pilgrim roads; long ago, thousands of pilgrims from northern Europe would pour down these roads, on their way to pay homage at the tomb of St Peter. They would cross the Alps via the Great Saint Bernard Pass, then – along the main trade road of the day, known variously as the Via Francigena or the Via Romea, indicating the two terminuses – they would descend along the Valle d'Aosta and pass through Turin. Here the route split in two;

there was a Ligurian road and a Po valley road. Those two routes ran together again at the Tuscan border, and the pilgrim road ran south to Lucca and Siena, and then on to Viterbo and, finally, Rome. In Tuscany, the places that can be identified in the mediaeval

accounts are Massa, Pietrasanta, Camaiore, Lucca, Altopascio, San Miniato, Certaldo, San Gimignano, Poggibonsi, Colle di Val d'Elsa, Monteriggioni, Siena, Buonconvento with the nearby abbey of Sant'Antimo, San Quirico d'Orcia, and Radicofani. All of these towns, to greater or lesser degrees, preserve significant structures and landmarks from the Middle Ages, but two in particular – San Gimignano and Siena – can truly claim to be daughters of the pilgrim road, and in a sense therefore, descendants of the entire European continent. Perhaps we can extend that concept to cover the entire route; travellers from outside of Italy may be able to recognize names of saints from their homelands in the Italianized dedications of many churches: San Remigio, San Moderanno, San Broccardo, San Marziale, San Martino, San Genesio; in many of these churches, the sculpture and the furnishings are typical of styles found north of the Alps. Let us consider San Gimignano, then. The town grew at the side of the Via Francigena, largely as a marketplace for the agricultural produce of the surrounding countryside. The centre of San Gimignano extended along the pilgrim road; the Romanesque collegiate church and numerous hostels for wayfarers were erected, and in short order the town had grown to a size that, in other European countries of that period, would have

A Tuscan landscape, where the few signs of a human presence are quickly lost among the slopes (preceding pages).

The jagged and fascinating Crete of the Siena area.

Vineyards of Tuscany.

qualified it to be a major city. The road giveth, and the road taketh away, to paraphrase the Bible: when the pilgrim road shifted its route, due to larger political considerations of a changing Italy, San Gimignano slowly but surely withered away forcing a halt to construction and growth. This marked the end of San Gimignano's prosperity, but it also meant the preservation of the mediaeval town bristling with towers, as if it had been trapped in amber. The same can be said of Siena. In ancient times, this was a Roman colony,

and not a very large one; in fact not much survives from its earliest period. Siena's great monuments, however, ranging from the cathedral to the Palazzo Pubblico, date from the prosperous time of the Via Francigena. Siena grew along that road until it became one of the largest towns in Europe. The earliest city centre, with the solemn cathedral and the enormous Spedale di Santa Maria della Scala, a mediaeval hospital, developed along the roadway, and growing out tangentially were the two "terzi" – thirds, instead of quarters – of Città and San Martino. An exquisite fresco by Ambrogio Lorenzetti in the Palazzo Pubblico, *Il buon governo in città e in campagna*, depicts the prosperity fostered in town and country by wise government; it also offers a remarkable peek at life in the Siena of the 14th century, crowded with wayfarers, peasants, and fine lords on horseback. The Via Francigena, in short, offers a glimpse of settings and atmospheres that have survived intact over the centuries. Following this route will also give the visitor, who may wish to abandon Romanesque monuments for a spell, a chance to see artistic centres dating from other periods of history. A short detour will take you to Volterra, abounding in mediaeval

monuments but also in archeological museums and landmarks from its time as an ancient Etruscan town. Another will bring you to Pienza, the birthplace of a great pope, Pius II, who renovated his native village, transforming it into an "ideal city" as theorized by Renaissance Humanist culture. Nearby is Monte Oliveto Maggiore, with its remarkable frescoes, a masterpiece of the Italian Renaissance. And, lest those who love Florence complain, a quick side trip to the Oltrarno, where pilgrims certainly passed. After touring the art collection of Palazzo Pitti, you can climb up through the extraordinary setting of the Boboli Gardens, to the panoramic ramparts of the Forte di Belvedere. Or you may choose to drive through the towns of the Florentine hills – Fiesole, Settignano, and Maiano – where you will see sights described in ecstatic terms by non-Italian visitors in the 19th century.

The abbey of Sant'Antimo, a major way-station along the Via Francigena.

The towers of San Gimignano still spread a mediaeval atmosphere over the town.

A steep stairway runs from the baptistery to the Piazza del Duomo in Siena.

Artists and Craftsmen of Florence's Oltrarno

A working-class neighbourhood across the river Arno, long ago the site of religious communities whose immense estates, with the mushrooming growth of Florence, slowly gave way to a dense settlement of row houses, extending backwards, their narrow facades overlooking the street. Beginning in the Middle Ages, this neighbourhood was called the Oltrarno; various manufacturing activities began to gravitate to the quarter, and wool especially was processed, spun, and woven here. Many were the workshops and factories. The Oltrarno truly became the centre of the important wool trade of Florence in the 15th century, when the great woolens fair, originally held in Piazza della Signoria, was moved to the area before the convent of Santo Spirito, Oltrarno's chief landmark. It is no accident, then, that construction should have begun on the church of Santo Spirito, adjoining the convent, in precisely that period. Filippo Brunelleschi began work in 1444; he was fresh from the gruelling experience of erecting a dome on the cathedral of Santa Maria del Fiore; once again he met Florence's expectations, creating one of the purest architectural gems of the Renaissance.

A radical change came when Luca Pitti, a Florentine banker and merchant, decided around 1450 to build a sumptuous palace in Oltrarno. Pitti was trying to keep pace with the rapidly rising Medici family, but his own waning fortunes forced him to call a halt to construction on his new palazzo. The half-finished Palazzo Pitti was purchased by none other than the Medici; a century later, Cosimo I de' Medici made it his ducal residence. For the Oltrarno this was a tremendous shift in status, from outlying area to thriving centre. The mediaeval Via Maggio thus became one of the most luxurious streets in Florence. The best architects of their day competed in building houses along it. After six generations of Medici, Palazzo Pitti came into the possession of the House of Lorraine; the new ducal family completed the Galleria Palatina, a particularly fine princely art gallery of the 17th and 18th centuries. To astound visitors even more, the Boboli Gardens were added, extending behind Palazzo Pitti up the hill of the same name; in this remarkable Italian-style garden, architecture and nature merge to form an open-air museum of great charm. Towering overhead is the Forte di Belvedere, built in 1590 as part of the town's defenses. In the middle of an esplanade in the fort is a small mansion, now used for art exhibitions. From the fort's walls, you have a fine view of all Florence. In time, your gaze will return to the Oltrarno, from which you have just climbed. You feel as if you have missed major monuments, such as the church of the Carmine, with the frescoes by Masaccio and Masolino, to name only the most important one. Just one good reason to return to this working-class neighbourhood, so dear to the Florentine authors of the 20th century, and not only because of its fine art. In Oltrarno, the genuine Florentine spirit still lives on.

The river Arno and the Ponte Vecchio as evening falls on the city of the Medici (facing page).

The church of Santo Spirito, emblem and fulcrum of life in Oltrarno.

A view of the Boboli Gardens.

The Forte di Belvedere.

Colle di Val d'Elsa, a Town of the Middle Ages

Colle di Val d'Elsa has an ancient pedigree: the earliest reliable documents attesting its existence date from the late 12th century. Even so, the castle of Piticciano, believed to be the original core of the town, is mentioned in a document dated 1007, and thus was probably built before the year 1000. That much is speculation; what we do know for certain is that Colle di Val

Nova, a fine work of 16th-century military architecture. The Borgo is a long narrow quarter, twisting and turning, lined by noble palazzi of the 16th and 17th centuries; consider in particular the Palazzo Usimbardi and Palazzo Buoninsegni, and the unfinished but magnificent Palazzo Campana, which marks the end of the Borgo. An archway forms the entrance

d'Elsa was a way station on the Via Francigena, the great trade road to France and the rest of Europe. Midway between San Gimignano and Siena, Colle di Val d'Elsa enjoyed the custom of pilgrims from all over the continent on their way to Rome. This was a sort of primeval tourist trade, contributing to the already prosperous economy based largely on farming. The town of Colle di Val d'Elsa comprises three levels. The Borgo, or old town (223 m) and the Castello, or castle (215 m), stand atop the last outcrop of the highland of the Grazie, and constitute the Colle Alta, or high hill. The Piano, or level area (130 m), forms the Colle Bassa, or low hill, a more modern section of the town. To climb up to the Borgo, you will pass through the impressive gate of Porta

to the Castello, a picturesque cluster of buildings. The quarter as a whole is as interesting as any of the individual buildings; it presents a blend of mediaeval architecture, in the smaller constructions, and 15th- and 16th-century architecture in the noble palazzi. The main thoroughfare of the quarter is the Via del Castello, lined by the most impressive buildings: the Palazzo Pretorio, which now houses the Museo Archeologico, or archeological museum; the cathedral, built in 1603-19 on the site of the Romanesque parish church of Sant'Alberto; the Palazzo Vescovile, or bishop's palace, which now houses the noteworthy Museo di Arte Sacra, or museum of religious art; the Palazzo dei Priori, with the Museo Civico and its collection of fine art. Toward the

end of the street and the Castello, where mediaeval towers and houses crowd together more densely, is the birthplace of Arnolfo di Cambio, the great sculptor and architect who died in Florence in 1302. And surrounding every notable monument here is a close-packed grid of mediaeval buildings, narrow stone lanes, stairways, leading to the overlooks and high walls above the upper Val d'Elsa. It is all like a giant stage setting of times gone by.

A view of Colle di Val d'Elsa (facing page).

The fortifications of the town, relics of a distant past.

A glimpse of the Middle Ages in Colle Alta.

The Tranquillity of the Abbey of Monte Oliveto Maggiore

In the Middle Ages, pilgrims leaving Siena on their way south toward Rome found themselves crossing a broad land of bare, clay-coloured hills, known as the "Crete." In late summer, after the harvest, these clay hills glittered white as bones in the bright Tuscan sunlight, a setting that still astonishes the wayfarer with its vastness and silence. It seems natural, then, that in 1313 one of these solitary and unwelcoming areas, called the "desert of Accona", should have appealed to a man sick of comfort and wealth, in search of spiritual asceticism. Bernardo Tolomei was a renowned professor of law and a member of one of Siena's wealthiest and most respected families. In his search for spirituality, he assembled a community that practiced the Rule of St Benedict; the community was recognized in 1319 as the Congregation of Monte Oliveto. In the following year, construction began on what became the vast religious complex that now stands, a haven for prayer and contemplation, but also a fecund hothouse of culture and art over the centuries. You enter the great abbey of Monte Oliveto Maggiore by passing through a fortified mediaeval gate-house; this simple square structure is no longer needed to protect the convent against brigands, but it still serves to admonish visitors to leave all worldly vanities behind them as they cross the threshold. Beyond is an oasis of peace and tranquillity that immediately prompts a respectful silence. A broad avenue lined with tall cypress trees leads down toward the centre of the complex. The botanical garden of the monastic apothecary and a 16th-century fish pond conjure up scenes of the industrious everyday life of the Benedictines. You then reach the handsome Gothic church, with its

facade adorned with an elegant portal; to your right is the main entrance to the monastery. Just beyond stands the Chiostro Grande, or Great Cloister. On the walls are 15th- and 16th-century frescoes of stories from the life of

St Benedict. There are 36 scenes portrayed; it is hard to decide which are the finest: St Benedict leaving his father's home to study in Rome, with a remarkably detailed view of his home town of Norcia; the scene in which the saint welcomes two Roman youths, Maurus and Placidus. This latter scene, in a monumental setting, is particularly masterful in its composition. Note that the figures, separated into two groups, have the features of leading figures of the period. The first to work on these frescoes was Luca Signorelli, a student of Piero della Francesca; later, Sodoma completed the frescoes before going on to work in the Vatican. Certainly, these frescoes are one of the major creations of the Italian Renaissance.

A detail of the frescoes of the stories of St Benedict (facing page).

A broad view of the abbey complex.

The Renaissance style can be glimpsed in the frescoes in the choir.

Pienza, an "Ideal City" of the Renaissance

Odd flukes of nature have preserved in fossil form the images of primordial creatures, trapped in geological strata or clumps of amber; likewise, the course of history has cemented in a noble Tuscan piazza the utopian Renaissance dream of the "ideal city." The piazza in question stands at the centre of an unassuming village, originally called Corsignano; in the Middle Ages, the town was a possession of Siena, and the feud of the Piccolomini family. Here, in 1405, Enea Silvio Piccolomini was born. He became a great humanist, poet, and statesman, and in time took the papal tiara and the name of Pius II. Immediately, he decided to transform his native village into a town worthy of a pontiff; he commissioned Bernardo Rossellino, the great Renaissance architect and sculptor, to do the job. Work began in 1459, and just three years later had advanced to the point that the pope raised Corsignano to the status of "città," or city, giving it a new name that would leave no one in doubt as to its allegiance: Pienza, as if to say "city of Pius II." The reconstruction was respectful of the original mediaeval buildings and layout; it was the centre that changed most, with new palazzi in a single uniform style, designed especially with a view to perspective and architectural details. The focal point of the entire project was the lovely Piazza Pio II: the first building erected on this square was the cathedral, with its Renaissance facade and, inside, three aisles, equal in height and breadth, in accordance with a plan typical of German Gothic. Next came the papal palace, based on the Palazzo Rucellai in Florence, designed by Leon Battista Alberti, with a stately three-fold set of loggias, and a hanging garden with a sweeping view of the Val d'Orcia, Radicofani, Monte Amiata, and Montalcino. Later, Pius II "persuaded" various cardinals and private citizens to build their own houses here: among them was the residence of Cardinal Rodrigo Borgia, who in turn became pope, with the name of Alexander VI. When both the pope and the architect died in 1464, work on Pienza – still unfinished – slowed, and the town reverted to the sleepy provincial life of before. This lethargy proved providential, however, as progress left no marks on the venerable square, which remains one of the most vivid surviving images of the "ideal city," a sanctuary of the Humanist ideal through the centuries.

Pienza, a mediaeval village, was made a city in the 15th century (facing page).

The interior courtyard of Palazzo Piccolomini, the home of Pope Pius II.

The stairway that leads up to the cathedral offers views of the Val d'Orcia.

Exquisite capitals embellish the loggias of the courtyard of Palazzo Piccolomini.

The tower that looms over Piazza Pio II.

From the Apennines to the Adriatic Beaches

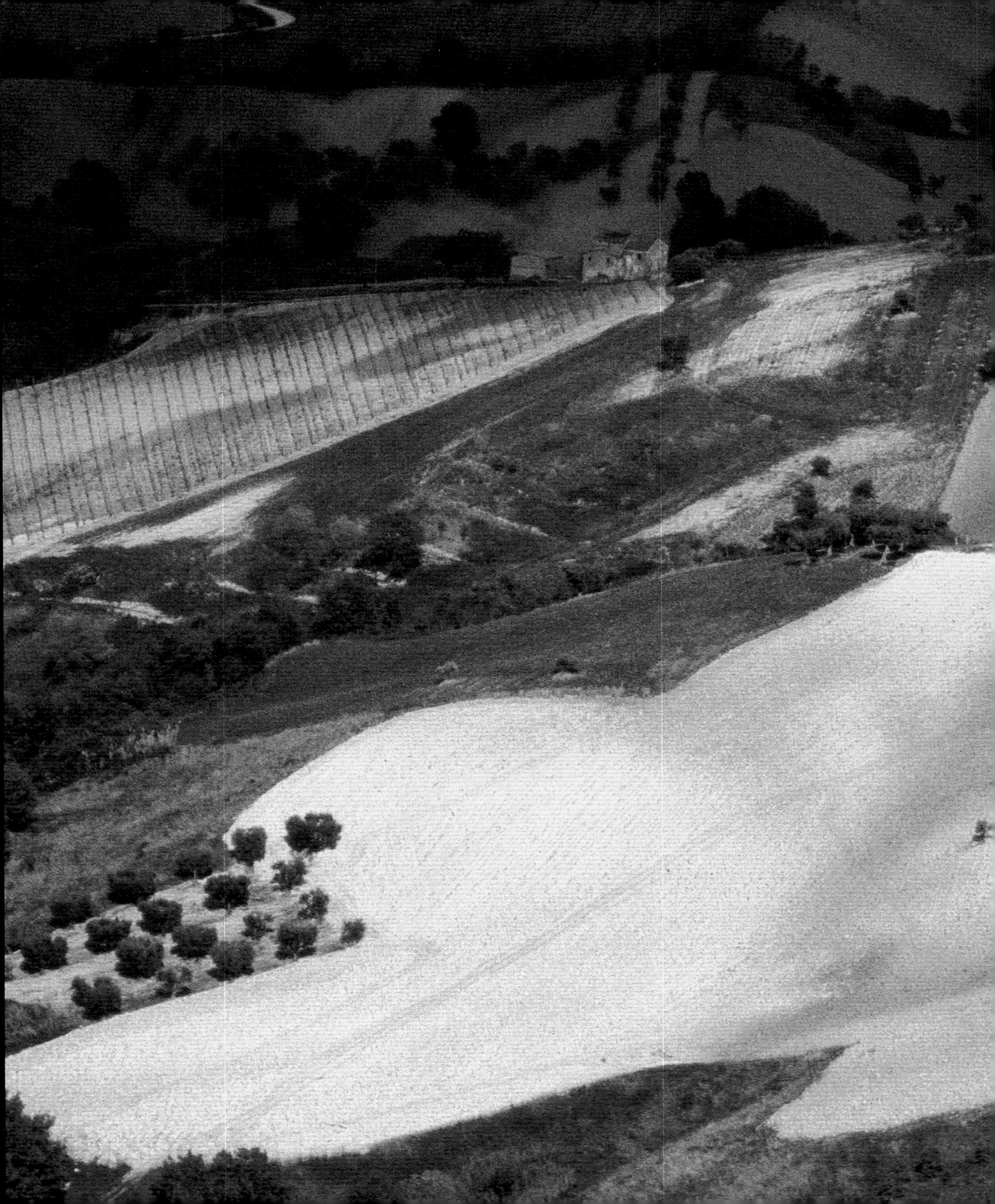

From the Heart of the Apennines to the Adriatic Beaches

If we draw a giant X connecting the four tips of the Italian peninsula, we will find that the cross-hairs line up square on the Monti Sibillini, in the lofty heart of the Apennines. These mountains mark the great divide between the Adriatic and the Tyrrhenian seas. The views are spectacular in both directions: to the west, they overlook the Umbrian uplands, hemmed in on all sides by wooded mountains; to the east, on the

other hand, they survey a boundless expanse of low, rolling rises, covering most of the Marches. This last notion – that the Marches are largely hilly – may surprise many, since the region is mainly thought of as a coastal region, devoted to the sea. It is not, in fact, well known that the most characteristic features of this territory are the hills: a distinctly agrarian landscape, and, despite the advent of mechanization, the landholdings laid out much as they were in ancient times, revealing the painstaking, canny craftsmanship of the peasants of the Marches. Set in this giant warp-and-weft of human labour

are the ancient towns of the Marches, surveying the valleys below; the abbeys and the country churches. Running from the base of these foothills is the long, broad strip of Adriatic coastline. This strip of littoral is sandy for long stretches; broken intermittently by the mouths of numerous watercourses, running – with unpredictable dry spells – down to the sea. Many small fishing towns sprang up long ago at these river mouths; more recently, tourist resorts have begun to appear as well. The only striking break in the low Marches coastline is Monte Conero – an island

in remote prehistory – which has worn down to the shape of a broad-backed whale, preparing to submerge.
Its seaside slopes are steep, plunging down to the water; its inland slopes taper gently down to the surrounding farmland. On the northernmost slopes lies Ancona, capital of the Marches, and the only natural harbour in the mid-

Adriatic, which is traditionally oriented toward the Greek and Slavic coasts. It comprises two clearly defined sections: old Ancona, with its monuments and works of art, and modern Ancona, dating only from the 18th century. Although Ancona has suffered bombardments and earthquakes, the historical centre, with its maze of busy narrow lanes, still has the flavour of an ancient seaport. While the gaze of the connoisseur will immediately fix on the church of San Ciriaco, a Romanesque masterpiece, Ancona offers myriad other jewels of fine old architecture:

The gentle slopes of the hills of the Marches (preceding pages).

A Romanesque-Gothic cathedral looms over the town of Fermo.

Monte Conero plunges into the sea at Sirolo.

The 14th-century walls of Gradara.

A monumental fountain in the piazza at Pesaro, the cradle of fine majolica, near the border with Romagna.

The Swabian castle in Termoli, a busy fishing and tourist port on the Adriatic Sea.

Trajan's arch, the church of Santa Maria della Piazza, and many mediaeval and Renaissance palazzi. There are other towns along this stretch of the Adriatic coastline with similar histories. One of these is Pesaro, with notable mediaeval, Renaissance, and Baroque monuments, and a distinguished tradition of fine majolica.

Other such towns include Fano, a Roman town abounding in monuments and ruins and Senigallia, a beach resort said to have "velvety sand." Inland, there are many towns with world-class castles and fine art. Foremost among them is Urbino, which has magically remained much as it looked in the second-half of 15th century, when the dukes of Montefeltro summoned the greatest painters and architects of the Renaissance to their magnificent court. Ascoli-Piceno, on the southern boundary of the Marches, is a stern monumental town, as notable for its remarkable location as for its profusion of palazzi, churches, towers, lanes, and roads. Jesi was the birthplace of the Holy Roman Emperor Frederick II; the town is now better known for its remarkable Verdicchio wine than for its many monuments. Still, Jesi's Palazzo della Signoria and its 14th-century walls, its maze of mediaeval lanes and stairways, will cast the visitor into a reverie of long-ago times. Then let us consider Fabriano, with its stunning Piazza del Comune and its centuries-old history of fine paper manufacturing. Recanati, where the great poet Giacomo

Leopardi lived and wrote some of the loveliest verse in Italian literature, also has fine architecture and art collections. Next is Fermo, with its ancient centre in the Piazza del Popolo, lined with public buildings, and the airy esplanade of the Girfalco, with the Romanesque-Gothic cathedral standing in lonely grandeur. Then there is Loreto, dominated by the celebrated sanctuary of the Santa Casa, one of the greatest destinations for pilgrimages in Italy, with fine art and architecture. And finally Gradara, a remarkable village surrounded by a ring of 14th-century walls stretching – studded with towers – all the way up to the fortress. Or you can turn toward Corinaldo, which boasts one of the most spectacular rings of walls in the region, as well as a handsome historical centre. If the hilly Marches are usually thought of as a maritime region, precisely the reverse happens in Abruzzo. Here, you immediately think of the Gran Sasso and the Maiella, the mountains of the Apennines par excellence; but you tend to forget the 150 kilometres of coastline, with towns like Pescara, Ortona, and Vasto. This odd inversion may be due to school textbooks or famous poems drilled into our heads as children, but sadly many Italians think of Abruzzo as a land of shepherds, flocks, and wolves; and perhaps as the land of the famed Parco Nazionale, a preserve for the protection of endangered species. Much the same thing happens with the Molise; many Italians are surprised to learn it has an outlet on the sea. And that outlet is the handsome town of Termoli, with its 13th-century Swabian castle and massive Romanesque cathedral; this is where it is customary to take ship for the Apulian islands of the Tremiti.

The "Palace of Art" of Urbino

"Duke of Urbino, count of Montefeltro; victorious warrior; just, clement, and most magnanimous prince" – these words, engraved in the frieze of a building, apply to Federico II, who transformed Urbino into the "ideal city" so dear to Humanist thought.

The first step in this ambitious project was the construction of a royal palace worthy to serve as hallmark to so noble an undertaking. In the late 15th century, therefore, he built the superb palace that was fundamentally to change Urbino's appearance. Designed and begun by Luciano Laurana, the palace was a triumph of skill and contrivance over the roughness of the ground and the intricate challenge of combining two existing buildings into one. Laurana's brilliant solution was to base the new palace around a gracious central courtyard; the proud western facade, set between two lofty towers, gives the palace the appearance of a fortress. Inside, a monumental staircase – greatly admired by the 16th-century art historian Giorgio Vasari – leads up to the sumptuous main halls of the court of Urbino. Over the centuries, furnishings and decorations have been stripped away; the carved portals and ceilings, magnificent doors, and exquisite inlays remain, to give an idea of the stately splendour that once reigned here. Consider the names of the various halls: the vast, majestic Salone del Trono, or Throne Room; the Sala delle Veglie, literally, the Hall of Soirées, where the duke entertained and received guests; the Ala del Magnifico, or Wing of the Magnificent, where Giuliano de' Medici stayed as a guest; the Appartamento Realissimo, or residence of the duke; and the Studiolo, a small ducal study with passages linking it both to the Cappella

The spiral staircase leading up to the main floor of the Palazzo Ducale (facing page).

The palazzo shown in its urban context.

The *Flagellation*, by Piero della Francesca, is one of the masterpieces in the Galleria Nazionale.

del Perdono – a chapel with exquisite marble facing – and with the Tempietto delle Muse, a small temple of the Muses. The study, with adjacent chapel and neo-classical temple, seems a perfect metaphor for the blend of religious and worldly knowledge that typified the Humanism of the early Renaissance. Some of the most illustrious artists of the Renaissance worked here, creating a body of fine art that now forms the core of the collections of the Galleria Nazionale delle Marche, housed in this palace. Among the many paintings on display are Raphael's *Portrait of a Gentlewoman* also known as *La Muta*; *The Profanation of the Host* by Paolo Uccello; and the *Flagellation* and the *Madonna of Senigallia*, two masterpieces by Piero della Francesca. Once the Palazzo Ducale was complete, Federico II assembled in its splendid halls some of the finest minds of his time, finally achieving his long cherished ambition: to create a court that would foster the ideal man described by Baldassare Castiglione.

The Outstanding Fortifications of Corinaldo

There was a time, in the late-15th and the early-16th century, when the Marches were perhaps the most brutally pummeled lands in Italy. Florence, the Church, Venice, the Sforza of Lombardy, and many local warlords, including the Malatesta and the Della Rovere, were all fighting for possession of this region. The mightiest tormentor of them all, however, was Cesare Borgia, the son of Rodrigo Borgia, Pope Alexander VI, and the brother of Lucrezia Borgia. Cesare, a duke, and known as the Valentino, was pitiless in his constant striving for military control; his motto was "aut Caesar aut nihil," translating roughly as "either master or nothing."

It should hardly come as a surprise, then, that the Marches, from the Middle Ages onward, should have seen so much energy and wealth devoted to the construction of new fortresses and the reinforcement of existing castles. Much work was put into adapting crenelated walls to withstand cannon fire. Famed architects came here to build these castles and forts. Among them were the Florentine Sangallo family, Girolamo Genga from Urbino, and the great Francesco di Giorgio Martini. One notable castle is in Corinaldo, a hilltop town inland from Senigallia, set high on a ridge separating the rivers Nevola and Cesano. It was probably founded in the 5th century by refugees from the nearby town of *Suasa*, an ancient Roman settlement destroyed by the Goths led by Alaric. The town of Corinaldo was ruled by the Buscareto family until the notorious cardinal Albornoz, in the late 14th century, seized control of it. Corinaldo then fell under the sway of the Malatesta, who were succeeded by the Sforza; next it came under the rule of the Papal State

again. In 1517 Pope Leo X elevated it to township status, in recognition of a level of prosperity that was only to increase over the next two centuries. Corinaldo has what is surely the most spectacular ring of walls in the entire Marches region; its historical centre is also notable, and features many splendid palazzi. The walls, which have

a circumference of 900 metres, were first undertaken in 1366 and completed in 1484-90. The gates, mighty towers, and strong bastions of these walls are all located in strategic points; the battlements, loopholes, and defensive trapdoors are all state-of-the-art creations of Renaissance military architecture. Beyond the impressive Porta Nuova extends the intact historical centre, with a broad tree-lined square known as the Terreno, and the Piazza del Cassero, with the little church of the Suffragio, built within the last of the towers of the Cassero Sforzesco, or Sforza Donjon.

The intact 14th- and 15th-century town walls extend for nearly a kilometre (facing page).

Bird's-eye view of the old walled town.

The Pozzo della Polenta, an ancient well and a landmark in the everyday life of the town.

Ancona, a City of Romanesque Harmony

Ancona lies along the shores of the broad gulf that corresponds to a spur of Monte Conero, inland and to the south, about halfway up the coast of the Marches. Founded in the 4th century B.C. by settlers from the colony of Syracuse, in Magna Graecia, it fell under Roman rule a century later, acquiring military importance and enjoying prosperous trade with many cities of the eastern Mediterranean, Alexandria among them. These links with the Near East brought Christianity to Ancona earlier than in much of the rest of Italy. As a result, Ancona has a remarkable number of very old churches.

A crossroads between Byzantium and Rome, this capital of the Marches was also a cultural melting pot, and it spawned a powerful new style. Consider Ancona's cathedral, the

church of San Ciriaco, high atop the Colle Guasco; it stands on the foundations of an ancient temple, probably dedicated to Aphrodite Eupleia, protectress of mariners. In the 6th century, the first Christian church was built, a three-aisled basilica; it was rebuilt in the late 9th century, following a particularly destructive Saracen raid.

From the porch of the cathedral of Ancona, your gaze extends out over the Adriatic Sea (facing page).

Santa Maria della Piazza and detail of the frieze over the portal (above).

San Ciriaco – the harmonious blending of various architectural features.

Between the late 11th and the early 12th centuries, the church was enlarged, and given a Greek-cross plan; it was in this period that the church acquired the remarkable stylistic blend of Byzantine and Romanesque that we see today. The facade has two notable Romanesque-Gothic features: a porch, with carved lions bearing columns, and a portal with a deep embrasure and splendid sculpted decorations. Each arm of the transept stands atop a crypt, and is split into three aisles by lines of Roman columns with Byzantine capitals. The whole interior is a perfect composition of well balanced spaces and volumes. At the centre, supported by four stout pillars with decorated spandrels, is the twelve-sided dome.

Note the remains of the pluteus, the dwarf wall linking the columns at their base; by Master Leonardo, this fine piece of mediaeval sculpture features fine materials and rigidly symmetrical lines, hinting at Eastern influence. Another notable instance of this combination of styles can be seen in the church of Santa Maria della Piazza, built in the early 13th century, on the site of early Christian buildings dating from the 5th or 6th century (note the fragments of remarkable mosaic floors). On the facade of this Romanesque church is an exquisite marble facing by the Lombard Master Filippo who, to judge by the overall harmony, must also have supervised the sculpture as well as the composition of the facade. The finest and most original touch is the subdivision of the surface with a series of small superimposed blind arches, in which both the earlier, Byzantine-style reliefs and the figures in the lunette over the portal are set, as if in a delicate piece of jewellery.

99

The Glorious Palazzo dei Capitani del Popolo in Ascoli Piceno

At the base of Apennines, set at the confluence of the river Tronto and a tributary stream, Ascoli Piceno stands on high ground that was girdled by walls in earliest prehistory. The town was originally a stronghold of the Piceni, an ancient Italic tribe. It later became a thriving Roman town, a crossroads of trade in central Italy. In the Middle Ages, Ascoli Piceno grew prodigiously, though it remained within the orderly grid established by its first, Roman conquerors. It was the Romanesque architecture of the Middle Ages, however, that gave Ascoli Piceno the stern and monumental appearance that a modern visitor will see. In mediaeval Ascoli Piceno, there were towers, palazzi, and no fewer than 200 churches; many buildings survive from this period. The oldest site and historically the most important area in Ascoli Piceno is the Piazza dell'Arringo. Under Roman rule this was the Forum; it now features the Palazzo Comunale, or town hall, and the Duomo, or cathedral.

The centre and meeting-ground of modern Ascoli Piceno, however, lies in the nearby Piazza del Popolo, a broad rectangular plaza surrounded by handsome porticoed buildings, and dominated by the immense 13th-century Palazzo dei Capitani del Popolo, town hall from 1400 to 1564. It then became the administrative building of the papal government. The facade of this remarkable building features an immense portal. The portal is surmounted by a monument to Pope Paul III (1549). On one side of the square stands the magnificent Gothic church of San Francesco, simple and severe; it was begun in the mid-13th century, and not completed until three centuries later. The facade, overlooking

The 13th-century tower of the Palazzo dei Capitani dominates the central Piazza del Popolo (facing page).

A view of the arcades of the building, renovated during the 16th century.

A decorative detail of the portal; lively architecture in the cloister of the Gothic church of San Francesco.

the adjacent Via del Trivio, is made of travertine blocks; there are three elaborate portals in the Venetian style. The central portal in particular is richly decorated, and is surmounted by a large oculus. The side facing the Piazza del Popolo, however, is every bit as spectacular as the facade. It features both the refined Loggia dei Mercanti, a Renaissance addition, and an immense side portal, beneath a monumental statue of Pope Julius II. Here Julius is portrayed giving a benediction, but he is better known to history as a fierce warrior and a patron of the arts. You should note the rear of the church, where the apse, the two five-sided bell towers, and the jutting arms of the transept combine to form a spectacular setting; note the interplay of light and shadow and the remarkable use

of perspective. On the other side of the church extends the large square cloister, open to the street; note the handsome columns topped by dynamic round arches. Make your way back to the square, and, before setting off to explore the rest of Ascoli Piceno, stop for a drink or an espresso at the venerable Caffè Meletti, a remarkable piece of Art-Nouveau architecture.

101

Protecting the Environment: The Parco Nazionale d'Abruzzo

Adjacent to one of the most unspoiled and inaccessible regions of the Apennines – the Marsica – where spectacular peaks loom over dense forests, abounding in wildlife, the Parco Nazionale d'Abruzzo, or national park of Abruzzo, was once a royal hunting preserve. In the 1920s, it was set aside as a national park, to ensure the preservation of endangered species. This land is fertile and rich. Humans have long made use of the territory: first nomadic hunters, in prehistoric times, tracking big game; then herders, leading their flocks. Thus, this is not truly virgin wilderness; it is a landscape shaped by humans, but in an organic and harmonious manner. The park now protects a complete array of high- and mid-elevation mountain environments; there are peaks that tower over 2,000 metres. This vast territory largely features limestone peaks, twisted into a series of fascinating shapes by the weight of ancient glaciers and by the steady erosion of rain water and wind. The forest is dense, with beech trees that grow to enormous size and attain remarkable ages. There are splendid meadow flowers, including such rare species as gentian and orchids. Among the wildlife are the brown bear, which, miraculously, has survived in such close proximity to modern civilization, and the chamois, which is so distinctive

in this region that it has been accorded a separate scientific classification. Also inhabiting this park are the wolf, the otter, the golden eagle, and many other species. This park has afforded all these species a haven in which to repopulate, as well as a base from which to colonize various habitats reclaimed by a laudable government policy of environmental protection. Abruzzo stands first in Italy in terms of preserving its territory; more than 30 percent is under some form of

environmental protection. This is a courageous choice; and it has allowed the recovery not only of bears and chamoix, but also of humans. Consider the new generation of "mountain men" who have in many cases moved back here from the city, leaving jobs in factories, to work in or around the park. In fact, "agritourism" and "green tourism" are two new fields of occupation, as is organic farming. The towns of their fathers, in some cases, are returning to new life.

Chamoix have been repopulating the Apennines (facing page).

From Settefrati, on the gentle slopes of the Colle Cicciuto, you can enjoy broad views of the mountains in the park.

Among the protected species, chamoix high on a crag in Val Fondillo, and Apennine wolves.

In the Umbrian Valley and Roman Etruria

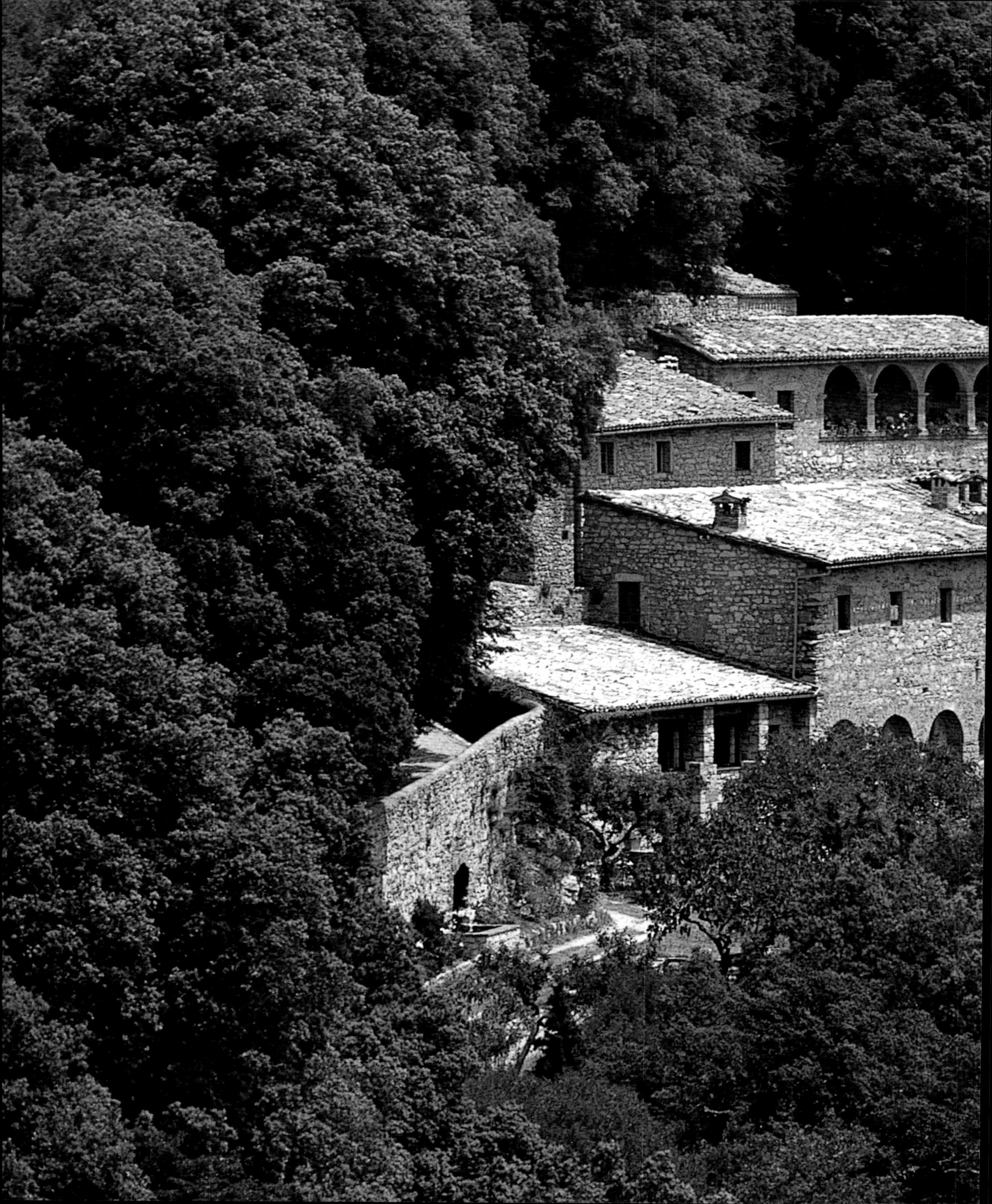

Spirituality and Power in the Umbrian Valley and Roman Etruria

Umbria is the "green heart" of Italy; the term perfectly describes its central, land-locked location, as well as its topography, almost entirely made up of mountains and wooded hills, watered by rushing torrents. This is the land of Francis of Assisi, the saint who sent a message of peace, brotherhood, and harmony with nature, throughout the Europe of his time and of ours. This treasure chest of spiritual values and meltingly lovely nature is known as the Valle Umbra, or Umbrian Valley; it stretches from the hilltop town of Perugia – with its Palazzo dei Priori and splendid collections of art – and the valley of the Tiber down to Spoleto. A broad plain in the shadow of Monte Subasio was the fit setting for the life of the saint who dedicated his life to poverty; indeed, Francis spent his life preaching and praying on the slopes of that mountain. You can still visit the Eremo delle Carceri, a sanctuary that

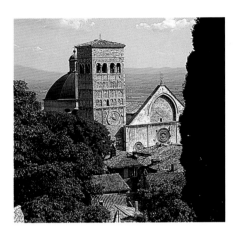

rose atop the original oratory founded by Francis and his earliest "brothers." Here the first Franciscan "incarcerated" themselves, leading a life of prayer and contemplation. On the mountain slopes, on one of the most picturesque and panoramic places in Umbria, stands the town of Assisi, where St Francis was born. His mortal remains are preserved in the Basilica di San Francesco here; this remarkable sacrarium of faith and art is decorated with frescoes by Giotto and Cimabue. There are many other monuments to the memory of this "santo poverello": the churches of San Damiano, Santa Maria di Rivotorto, and Santa Maria degli Angeli, to name only the most celebrated. So great is the power of these monuments and their history, that other remarkable landmarks – the cathedral, the temple of Minerva, the church of Santa Chiara, the Rocca Maggiore, or fort – may go unnoticed. This would be a pity.

To the SE of Assisi, the Valle Umbra offers a succession of handsome mediaeval villages and towns. A broad expanse of olive groves runs down to Spello, an ancient town with notable Roman, mediaeval, and Renaissance monuments – a town of charm and fine views of mountains and plains. Continuing along the fertile valleys of rivers that flow into the Tiber, you will pass through three towns – the first in the plain, the other two on

The Eremo delle Carceri, on the verdant slopes of Monte Subasio, is a silent witness to the life of St Francis (preceding pages); also, the cathedral of Assisi (top).

The Via alla Fortezza, in old Spello.

Perugia twinkles in the twilight.

Civita di Bagnoregio, threatened by the crumbling plateau on which it stands.

In Spoleto, architecture finds a fitting place in the views of the "green heart" of Italy.

The rose window of the Gothic church of Santa Chiara in Assisi, a circle of lace cut into marble.

the western slope of the valley – that are different in size and appearance, but all sharing a glorious history and artistic heritage.

First is Foligno, an up-to-date little

town, with shops and some manufacturing, the centre of the network of rail and road in Umbria; still, Foligno preserves handsome Renaissance architecture and fine art in its historical centre. Next comes Montefalco, in a magnificent panoramic setting, a town of noble mediaeval appearance. Particularly notable here are the major Tuscan and Umbrian frescoes in the churches of Montefalco. Last is Bevagna, at the foot of green hills, with a fascinating ancient atmosphere; in particular, note the silent Piazza Silvestri.

Further along, atop a cone-shaped hill overlooking the plain of Spoleto, we find Trevi, a lovely and interesting little town with fine art collections and beautiful surroundings. The Valle Umbra comes to a magnificent close with Spoleto, high atop a rise at the foot of the wooded Monteluco. It survives virtually intact. This town appears like a massive grey cluster atop the hill from a distance; from up close, you begin to sense its variety. There are pre-Roman and Roman walls, classical monuments, early Christian churches, Romanesque and Gothic architecture of all sorts. Clearly, Spoleto has always been an important and respected town; it now boasts the arts festival, "Festival dei Due Mondi," or Festival of the Two Worlds. Instead of heading straight for Rome, you may choose to detour onto the best road for exploring Roman Etruria, off the beaten tourist track. Viterbo, for example, is the historic capital of this territory. In its city centre is

the mediaeval Palazzo dei Papi and the charming quarter of San Pellegrino. Then, to cite only a few of the better known sites, consider Tarquinia, famous for its vast Etruscan necropolis; Tuscania, with two great Romanesque churches as a sign of its one-time wealth and power; Civita di Bagnoregio, a mediaeval "borgo," fast becoming a ghost-town, high atop a plateau that is slowly but surely crumbling away. Last, as you head toward Rome, you will see the great aristocratic residences that are in some cases fortresses – like the Castello Orsini in Bracciano – and in other cases sumptuous holiday homes, such as the Palazzo Farnese in Caprarola, with its refined architecture and ornate gardens, as if whetting your appetite for the wonders of eternal Rome.

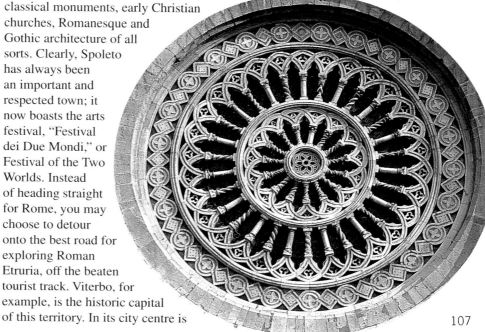

107

Perugia: The Imprint of the Middle Ages, Carved in Stone

The heart of mediaeval Perugia is the superb Piazza IV Novembre, surrounded by the town's finest buildings – Palazzo dei Priori and the cathedral, a cunning assemblage of asymmetrical volumes – and adorned by the Fontana Maggiore, a great 13th-century fountain. This fountain, a resplendent symbol of Perugia itself, was the joint effort of Nicola Pisano and his son Giovanni, undoubtedly the finest sculptor of the Gothic Italian style and a father of the Italian Renaissance. The Pisanos, father and son, had already created masterpieces in the cathedral of Siena and the baptistery of Pisa. Working with them were Fra Bevignate, a Benedictine monk who was later to supervise the construction of the cathedral of Orvieto, and Boninsegna Veneziano, a pioneer in the field of hydraulic engineering. Together, they created a masterpiece of the late Middle Ages: two concentric, polygonal marble basins, surmounted by a bronze bowl. The bottom basin is studded with bas-relief panels, bearing symbolic depictions of the months of the year, the signs of the Zodiac, and other allegorical themes. The upper basin features statuettes of biblical characters and figures from the history of Perugia. Set in the bronze bowl is a group of three nymphs bearing an amphora from which gushes a stream of water. Overlooking this fountain and the surrounding square is the proud Palazzo dei Priori, seat of mediaeval Perugia's government. Of the building's two facades, the one overlooking Piazza IV Novembre is the older; note the majestic fan-shaped staircase leading up to the great portal, beneath the lordly gaze of the Griffin, symbol of Perugia, and the Lion, symbol of the Ghibelline party, aristocratic mediaeval partisans

of the Holy Roman Empire. The later facade, on the Corso Vannucci, features a magnificent, round-arched portal, decorated as if it led into a great cathedral. Inside is the Galleria Nazionale Umbra, a great art gallery featuring work by such Umbrian and Tuscan masters as Fra Angelico, Piero della Francesca, Perugino, and Duccio di Buoninsegna.

Do not miss the remarkable pomp and splendour of the official halls in Palazzo dei Priori: the late-Gothic Collegio della Mercanzia, or headquarters of mediaeval Perugia's Guild of Merchants; the Sala dei Notari, or Hall of the Notaries, with vivid frescoes of Bible stories, alternating wit' scenes of history or everyday life and heraldic

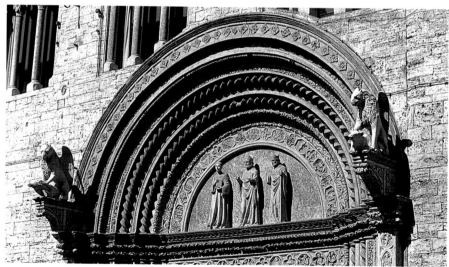

The splendid Fontana Maggiore was the creation of, among others, Nicola Pisano and his son Giovanni (facing page).

The Griffin, symbol of the Umbrian capital.

The portal of the Palazzo dei Priori invites you to imagine the past of the busy Corso Vannucci.

crests; the Collegio del Cambio, headquarters of the money-changers, was decorated by Perugino, who portrayed the great cultures of antiquity meeting the Christian spirituality of his time, with pagan deities and classical heroes side by side with characters from the Bible and portrayals of Christian virtues personified.

Franciscan Memories in Assisi

Assisi and St Francis. It is impossible to speak of this small Umbrian town at the foot of Monte Subasio without thinking of the humble man – Italy's patron saint – who preached to the birds, renounced his worldly wealth, and devoted his life to charity, brotherhood, and universal love, in the late 12th century. This quiet and snug little town, redolent of the ages, seems to cherish the sacred memory of Francis and his mystical companion, St Clare. The holiest spot in all Assisi, however, is the Basilica di San Francesco; construction began in 1228, two years after Francis's death. It was initially planned as an unassuming sepulchre, in the Franciscan spirit; in time it evolved into one of the most remarkable architectural monuments in all Italy, comprising two churches, one atop the other. This great church almost overshadows the surrounding town. The heart of the basilica is the crypt, where St Francis is buried. The small, unadorned chamber is the part of the church that most fittingly mirrors the soul of Francis of Assisi, who understood that the poor in spirit are particularly blessed. Outside of the crypt are the exquisite frescoes of the lower basilica, amid haunting low Gothic arches. From the darkness of the lower basilica one climbs up to the crescendo of light of the upper basilica, with its splendid series of frescoes by Giotto and his school, one of the greatest masterpieces of Italian art. The nearby church of Santa Chiara – St Clare – is simple and austere. From the centre of the broad nave is a little stairway that leads down to a crypt; here are enshrined the mortal remains of Clare, the mystical sister of Francis; her bones were discovered in 1850 beneath the main altar. In a chapel in this church is a 12th-century Crucifix, originally in the church of San Damiano; supposedly, this Crucifix spoke to St Francis in his youth, urging him to rebuild the church of San Damiano. And it is the church of San Damiano, perhaps more than any other place in Assisi, that best reflects the Franciscan spirit. Its walls are rough and dark, coloured here and there by frescoes. The long nave shrouded in shadows almost seems like a cavern more than a piece of architecture. Adjoining the church is the lovely cloister and the humble rooms where St Clare once lived. It was almost certainly here that St Francis wrote the *Canticle of the Sun*, a moving piece of religious poetry in praise of the Lord and His creation; particularly stirring when one considers that a suffering St Francis wrote it on his deathbed.

Quiet and meditation under the arches of the convent of San Francesco (facing page).

Night-time view of the basilica.

The poor saint in one of the frescoes by Giotto in the Basilica Superiore.

A stairway leads up to the church of San Damiano.

Tracking Down the Churches of Spoleto

The first thing that strikes you about Spoleto, as you look at it from a distance – a solid grey mass clustered on the hillside before you – is its remarkable variety, proud testimony to its extreme age and its continuing importance over the centuries. The building that best represents mediaeval Spoleto is the cathedral, erected in the late 12th century, on the ruins of an earlier cathedral, razed by Frederick I Barbarossa. In the centre of the facade, which is flanked by an impressive

bell tower, is a large Byzantine-style mosaic, surrounded by rose windows. Inside, note the frescoes by Pinturicchio, in the Cappella Eroli, and by Filippo Lippi, in the apse. As you leave the church, you immediately become aware that the mediaeval architecture of Spoleto is only the culmination of centuries of prior construction: note the impressive ancient Roman and pre-Roman ruins, and especially note two impressive buildings that mark the transition from the ancient world to the Middle Ages. The first is the church of San Salvatore, built at the turn of the 5th century; a remarkable building that has survived largely intact over the millennia; the facade originally resembled a classical temple, while the interior is that of a three-aisled early Christian basilica. This church hearkens back to ancient styles and structures; it aroused great interest among architects and artists of the Renaissance.

The second noteworthy building is the church of San Pietro fuori le Mura,

built in the high Middle Ages on the ruins of Roman buildings. Rebuilt as a Romanesque church in the 12th and 13th centuries, San Pietro was later heavily renovated. The facade, happily, was spared; note the remarkable decoration of this masterpiece of Umbrian Romanesque sculpture: ten large allegorical bas-reliefs in the lower order, the symbols of the four Evangelists surrounding the great rose window above, and statues of St Peter and St Andrew, and two sacrificial bulls, in the upper order.

The cathedral of Spoleto welcomes the visitor with its magnificent mosaic and the rose windows of its facade (facing page).

Virgin with Child, by Filippo Lippi, in the apse of the cathedral.

Columns on the interior of the church of San Lorenzo.

The facade of San Pietro fuori le Mura.

The Splendours of the Farnese

A century was all that was needed by the Farnese, an ancient family of feudal lords with lands west of Rome, to establish themselves in the Eternal City and there amass such enormous wealth and power that one of the clan was elected pope. This happened in 1534, when Alessandro Farnese became pope, with the name of Paul III. This was the crowning touch to a spectacular climb to power; the family decided to symbolise their achievements in spectacular buildings. Among the palaces and villas they

owned in the capital and elsewhere, the most remarkable is surely the one that was built on their lands at Caprarola. It was originally designed as a fortress, by Antonio da Sangallo the Younger, a pupil of Bramante. The Florentine architect conceived a great five-sided building; before work was even properly underway, the building was deemed too small for the Farnese, now one of the most illustrious and powerful dynasties in all Europe. The Farnese

no longer needed a common fortress; they required a magnificent monument. The original project was taken in hand by another Alessandro Farnese, great-grandson of Pope Paul III; this Farnese entrusted the job to the Vignola, who worked with Sangallo, the same Vignola who built the sumptuous church of the Gesù in Rome. The new architect made changes in the huge five-sided structure begun by his predecessor; his remarkable solution was to invert the urbanistic hierarchy of Caprarola, that is to say, to create

the illusion that the palazzo had not been added to the village, but rather that the village had been built around the palazzo. Thus, the building became the powerful centre of the town, and every view converged upon it. The Farnese residence stood high atop a series of impressive stairways, at the end of a long straight road. The architect further enhanced the illusion by raising this road above the uneven ground of the surrounding town,

as if it were a bridge running between two rows of sumptuous buildings to the great palace. And the conceit of this bridge must have impressed the refined intellectuals of the day. The destination of this obligatory passage was a circular courtyard in the centre of the building, with handsome portico and loggia – one of the most stunning creations of Italian architecture of the 16th century. Inside, a magnificent spiral staircase leads up to the main "noble" floor. Here, the visitor was obliged to admire the "Fasti Farnesiani," or "Farnese

Glories": a series of frescoes which offered a sort of "modern mythology" of the powerful family.

A view of Caprarola (facing page).

Note the trompe-l'œil columns (left) and the spiral staircase (right), details added by the Vignola.

In the frescoes of the "Fasti," or "Glories," the cardinal Alessandro Farnese with Francis I of France and Charles V.

Art and the Sea Under Mount Vesuvius

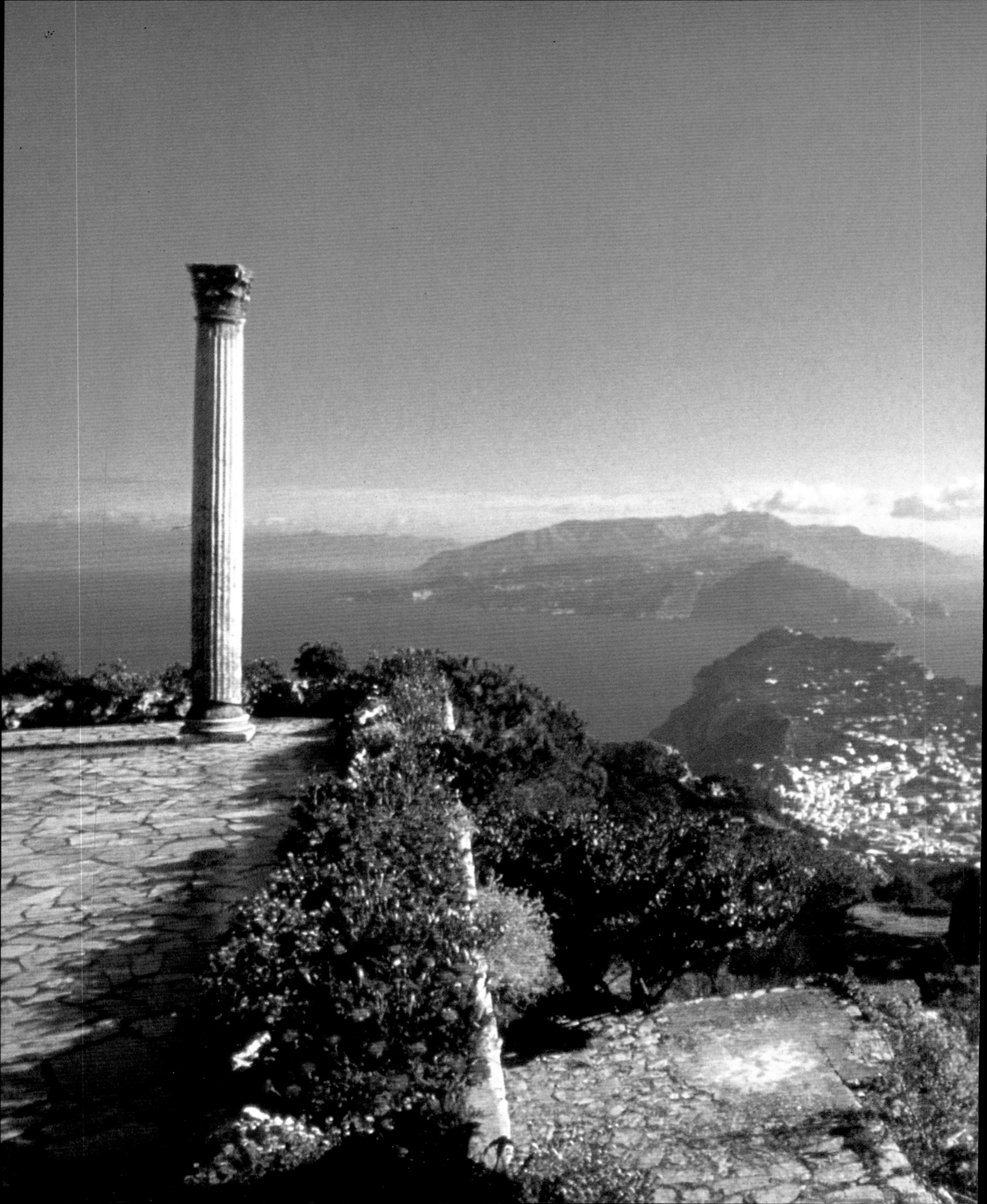

Art and the Sea Under Mount Vesuvius

A vast expanse of blue water, a series of volcanoes, high rocky coasts, a handful of islands... No, this is not Hawaii, nor is it Japan. The setting is a bit less exotic: the Bay of Naples, certainly the most fitting surroundings for Naples, the exuberant and fiery capital of Campania. A series of volcanoes? Well, first and foremost, of course, is Mount Vesuvius; this sleeping giant has been known to wreak tremendous havoc, like the one that buried Herculaneum and Pompeii 1,917 years ago. Currently, Vesuvius has retired – for the moment – and is now nothing more than a benign and scenic

backdrop. There are other volcanoes, however; perhaps we should say, there are the remains of other volcanoes. The Phlegrean Fields, antechamber to the Avernus, a land dotted with sulphureous fumaroles. Here is the Temple of Serapis, at Pozzuoli; the temple itself has become an "instrument of measurement" of

bradyseism, a geological term indicating the slow but detectable rise and fall of the land. We should also mention the island of Procida, and its larger neighbour, Ischia; the islands' hot springs and the conical mass of Ischia's Monte Epomeo indicate that, in the distant past, the two islands were part of an underwater volcano. In short,

surrounding the bay of Naples are the extinct remnants of a ring of volcanic craters; millions of years ago, they emerged from the waters of a much larger bay, which extended from the Monti Aurunci, to the north, down to the peninsula of Sorrento, to the south. Then the more active volcanoes, closer to the coastline, built up enough eruptive debris to join the mainland; the others became islands in the open sea. Besides the volcanoes, we should mention the steep rocky coasts of the peninsula of Sorrento, which offer the crowning touches to this great portrait of the Bay of Naples: the peninsula is actually a long ridge running down – in a series of spectacular formations – from the Apennines into the Tyrrhenian

Sea. Having plunged into the blue waters of the bay, it emerges once again as the island of Capri, its last and greatest gift to this region. These lovely places stand out in a region that the

From Villa Jovis on Capri, the gaze ranges out toward Sorrento (preceding pages).

The Tyrrhenian Sea and the Amalfi coast.

Night lights along the harbour of Naples.

The houses of Positano, high over the sea.

ancients highly esteemed. They called it *Campania felix*, and built villas and holiday palaces here. A mild climate, lovely settings, blue sea and hot springs: the ancients knew what they were doing. The Bay of Naples was far from the madding crowd of Rome; even back then, however, it was easy to reach. It became fashionable in the late Republic, thanks to the fact that "opinion-makers" of the period liked to holidayed here; among them were Marius, Crassus, Lucullus, Cicero, and Brutus. This area became a major holiday spot for the powerful of the Roman empire. The Gulf of Pozzuoli, and in particular the towns of Baiae, Miseno, and Bacoli, were the nerve centre of this privileged area. Also of importance was Sorrento, which stood across from them, on a terrace towering over the sea. And Tiberius actually established his residence on Capri during the last ten years of his life, ruling the empire with orders conveyed by a chain of signal towers. This was a time of wealth and luxury, about which we know many details due to the discovery of the excavation of Pompeii and Herculaneum. Here, under ashes and lava, were frescoed houses, so perfectly preserved that it seems you can hear echoes of banquets and entertainments. There was a second period of splendour around the year 1000, with the arrival of the Norman conquerors. These formidable "men from the north" were invited in as mercenaries; once they were here, they profited from the political confusion that reigned here, and built a unified and powerful state that included Sicily as well. Taking advantage of this new order were a number of cities, Salerno foremost among them. Salerno was for many years capital of the kingdom, and it even offered hospitality to the exiled Pope Gregory VII. In the mediaeval quarter of narrow winding streets, there are many eloquent reminders of the splendour of the Norman court, especially the cathedral with its superb

mosaics and the exquisite collections of religious art in the Museo Diocesano. Also dating from Norman times is the foundation of the Scuola Medica, the famous School of Salerno, an ancient and prestigious institute for the study of the Hippocratic sciences, pride of the city. The towns of the nearby peninsula of Sorrento also grew at prodigious rates. Amalfi, the earliest Italian maritime Republic, whose doges were

The village of Procida, on an island with a maritime tradition; midway to Ischia.

The Romanesque and the Moorish-Norman style mingle in the cathedral of Amalfi.

Atrani, where the nobles of Amalfi once had their homes.

crowned in nearby Atrani, whose white houses are scattered in picturesque disorder along the steep slopes; here covered lanes, narrow and lovely, like so many corridors of a convent, lead one to the discovery of remarkable relics from Norman times: the Duomo, with its multicoloured facade atop a high staircase, the enchanting Chiostro del Paradiso, a cloister with twin columns and braided arches; the impressive ruins of the arsenal; the former convent of the Capuchins, high overlooking the sea. Buildings with the Moorish style introduced by wealthy families of merchants with frequent contacts with Sicily. And then there is Ravello, said to have had a population of 36,000 in the 12th century. Clear signs of Ravello's great wealth can be seen in the many civil and religious buildings: the cathedral, Villa Rufolo, Villa Cimbrone, San Giovanni del Toro, and Santa Maria a Gradillo are just a few of the best

known monuments, but the town itself, even its less spectacular buildings, is the true museum of architecture. The coastline has, once again, become a holiday spot. Here a traveller who knows how to escape the throngs of tourists may find secluded places of incomparable beauty.

Pozzuoli and the Phlegrean Fields: Where Myth and History Merge

The narrow, semicircular arc of the Gulf of Pozzuoli is the source of many of the darkest and most deep-rooted myths of Greek and Roman culture: here, pious Aeneas landed in his flight from Troy, as did Greek Ulysses on his long, homeward quest; here thunder-wielding Jupiter battled the Giants; here was the entrance to the Underworld and Charon, the mythical ferryman of souls; here the sibyl of Cumae was worshipped. This land abounding in myths is the product of volcanic activity. It stands atop an underground caldera; visit the Solfatara, and everywhere you will see fumaroles and tiny mud volcanoes. As if the land were breathing, it swells and sinks, an example of what geologists call

---

The Flavian Amphitheatre, a clear indication of the prosperity that Pozzuoli once knew (facing page).

The grotto of the sibyl of Cumae.

The Solfatara of Pozzuoli is still a passageway for primeval forces of earth.

The Serapaeum of Pozzuoli.

"bradyseism." Proof of this bradyseism can be found in one of Pozzuoli's ancient Roman monuments. Long thought to be a sanctuary of the Graeco-Egyptian god Serapis, it was actually a market place, consisting of a broad portico with 36 shops. The shafts of the columns that still stand throughout this huge archeological park show marks of holes left by rock-boring sea mollusks, unequivocal proof that they were once underwater. The volcanism of the Phlegrean Fields is also the cause of one of their greatest attractions: the hot springs. Spas and thermal baths

made this one of the favourite resort areas of ancient Romans, in the late Republic and throughout the Empire. This splendid and fashionable holiday spot certainly attracted Cicero, who wrote *De republica* here; Pompey came here on holiday with his sons; Julius Caesar came here to rest body and soul following the Gallic Wars.

Some sense of the lavish splendour that once reigned here can be had among the ruins of the Imperial Palace of Baiae, so vast that they were once thought to be the remains of three separate temples, dedicated to Diana, Mercury, and Venus. In nearby Bacoli,

there are ruins of sumptuous seaside villas, where the great and powerful of the time came to rest and to play; so lascivious and decadent was the living here that both Seneca, the philosopher, and Propertius, the poet, decried it. A far different atmosphere prevails in the most famous spot in Cumae: the grotto of the sibyl. An almost oppressive fascination surrounds this underground sanctuary; this tour of part of Campania thus ends with a return into the bowels of the Earth, to the hidden sulphureous soul of a world hovering between myth and history.

Pompeii, Buried by Nature and Preserved by Time

In 79 A.D. – in the last days before the tremendous eruption – Vesuvius was a verdant mountain covered with vineyards; Pompeii was a prosperous Roman city at the mountain's base. The Pompeiians themselves were merchants and manufacturers; they lived in lovely homes and enjoyed socializing and luxury. We can still see atria, colonnades, gardens with fountains and statues, elegant halls and heated baths, friezes, mosaics, and frescoes. This world of comfort and wealth was frozen in time when Vesuvius exploded with the force of a hundred atomic bombs and buried Pompeii in lava, ashes, and mud.

In many rooms, excavated over the past two-and-a-half centuries, you have the impression that you can still hear the cheerful echoes of those banquets which were the chief social events of those ancient days. In the largest mansions, there was a special banqueting room – the *triclinium* – usually furnished with three couches, each large enough to hold up to three reclining guests; the precept was that

a banquet should involve guests "no fewer in number than the three Graces, no greater than the nine Muses." Dishes were served on portable tables. Juvenal describes one such banquet: "An enormous lobster with a side dish of asparagus, a Corsican mullet, the finest lamprey eels from the Strait of Messina, a goose liver, a capon the size of a house, a steaming roast pig, truffles..." It should come as no surprise that banquets of such abundance should degenerate into something orgiastic, with elements of esoteric religious cults. Splendid evidence of this comes from the series of frescoes that decorate the triclinium of the Villa dei Misteri, or Villa of Mysteries. The great painting depicts the presentation of brides to the Dionysian "mysteries," i.e., the cult of the god of wine and transport. It is believed that the mistress of the villa was a priestess in this cult. Consider that the Roman senate levelled serious penalties to halt the excesses that resulted from the introduction of this eastern religion; then imagine the embarrassment of the first archeologists, in the 18th century, to excavate in Pompeii. An aura of superstition came to settle around this buried city; many narrow minds interpreted the eruption and ensuing catastrophe as a divine judgment against the dissolute lives that were led here.

The volcano preserved ancient shops for posterity (facing page).

"Dionysiac" frescoes in the Villa dei Misteri.

An ancient road in Pompeii.

The house of the Fontana Grande.

The Romantic Enchantment of Ravello

At the height of its power, in the 13th century, the town of Ravello is said to have had a population of 36,000. Ravello was a port of the first order; one clear symbol of its former wealth and might is the cathedral of San Pantaleone, high atop a long flight of stairs, with its glittering bronze doors and two marble pulpits, decorated with mosaics.

Ravello's great wealth also appears in the many civic edifices and, especially, private residences built in the Sicilian-Arabic style. This style of construction was introduced by the rich families that traded with Sicily and the East.

One such luxurious home is the Villa Rufolo, a lovely cluster of buildings standing just SE of the cathedral, on a high terrace (350 metres above sea level) overlooking the gulf of Salerno. To enter the grounds, you must pass through a gate set in a 14th-century tower; you will then walk along a cypress-lined lane to the villa itself. The heart of the villa is a courtyard with two loggias featuring graceful, slender columns. The villa stands in a garden of Mediterranean and exotic plants; nearby are evocative ruins. Richard Wagner, who toured the villa on 26 May 1880, compared it to the dreamlike magical garden of Klingsor in his *Parsifal*. In recognition of this visit, *Parsifal* is performed here every summer. Not far off, at the southernmost tip of the spur on which Ravello stands, is the Villa Cimbrone, with an equally ineffable air to it. Here, alluring buildings are surrounded by enchanting nature: the vast, lovely garden abounds in blooming rosebushes, camellias, and hydrangeas, and many other exotic species. At the end of a long, statue-lined alley, the Cimbrone belvedere overlooks an unrivalled panorama. Further down are the Belvedere di Mercurio, the Grotto of Eve, the little Temple of Bacchus, the Rose Garden, and the pavillion of the Sala da Tè, or tearoom: enchanting spots adorned with artistic creations. But, here too, the absolute centre of attention remains the Amalfi coast, enchanting travellers from all over the world, as it has for generations.

The Belvedere di Mercurio in Villa Cimbrone (facing page).

The carved lions supporting columns under a pulpit in the cathedral (top left); a marble *Agnus Dei* (right) in the Museo del Duomo.

Sculpture and architecture in Villa Cimbrone, with a spectacular setting.

Elegant arches in Villa Rufolo.

Capri, Legends and Loveliness

Capri was long thought to be the island of the Sirens. In the *Odyssey*, Ulysses had his sailors plug their ears with wax; he alone heard the Sirens' song, lashed to the mast lest he succumb to their fatal lure. He seems to have been alone in history in his obstinate reluctance to land on Capri. The emperor Augustus, for instance, traded the much richer island of Ischia to the Greek town of *Neapolis*, or Naples, in exchange for Capri, then called *Capreae*. The emperor Tiberius, went so far as to build twelve villas on the island, each dedicated to a different deity of Olympus; he then took up residence in the largest villa of them all, the Villa Jovis. We moderns are as enthralled by Capri's charms as the ancients were; centuries of invasions, incursions, and pirate raids, and more recent and modern blights and plagues have done little to lessen the island's allure. Forgotten for centuries, and noted only for its fine wines and the seasonal hunts of migrating quail, Capri came back into vogue in the 1830s, when Hans Christian Andersen, the Danish author, and a Nordic poet named Kopisch astonished Europe with heartfelt descriptions of the island's loveliness. The Romantic sensibility, encouraged by the mythical figures hovering over the grottoes and ruins, brought tourism back to Capri. In the one-and-a-half centuries that have passed since then, the "Island of the Sirens" has attracted visitors of every ilk: crowned heads and royalty without a throne; oil barons, coffee kings, archeologists, composers, and writers; sophisticated adventurers and crass builders and developers. All Capri's visitors sooner or later passed through the Piazzetta, centrepiece of the island. The Palazzo Cerio has housed such royals as Czar Nicholas II, the

Austro-Hungarian emperor Franz Josef, and Victoria, queen of Sweden. The Casa Rossa was the elegant residence of Gorky, who offered hospitality to various Russian exiles, including Lenin. Many famous names have graced the registers of the many historic hotels. Note the dizzying Via Krupp, built by an heir to the German steel fortune as a token of a great passion. Note also the Villa San Michele, home of Axel Munthe, a Swedish court physician who retired to Capri, where he wrote *The Story of San Michele*, which made the island a legend. Despite all this frenzied partying and development, socializing and maneuvering, you will still find plenty of the wonders of nature

The switchback curves of the Via Krupp, a dizzying pedestrian path (facing page).

The Faraglioni of Capri, cliffs that have long been world-famous.

On the "Island of the Sirens," white houses cling to the steep slopes.

that so entranced the ancients: broad vistas in which the signs of the present fade away, sea floors studded with corals and lush in underwater plant life, mountain slopes blanketed in lilies and orchids, soaring seagulls and peregrine falcons. Everything still seems to be in its place; only the Sirens are missing.

Landscapes and Men of Puglia and the Basilicata

In the 19th century, schoolteachers told generations of Italian pupils that Italy was a "boot," Puglia constituting both the "spur" and the "heel" of that giant boot. In geological terms, the metaphor may have been less than scientific, but the schoolchildren learned the proper shape of Italy, and were never to forget it. And on one point, at least, those schoolteachers were right: the rocky Gargano promontory is indeed a spur, and not only in shape. This limestone headland juts eastward out into the Adriatic Sea, ruffle meadows dotted with orchids, and toss the branches of dense lovely woods. This portrait of the Gargano is completed by a list of fine coastal towns, Vieste, Peschici, and Rodi Garganico, and Monte Sant'Angelo, the highest town on the promontory. Here stands the sanctuary of San Michele Arcangelo, once a major way-station for pilgrims and crusaders on their way to the Holy Land. It was here that the rebel leader Melo, just after the year 1000, made his fateful appeal to the Normans to help his land break free of the Byzantine yoke. Unknowingly, he triggered the Norman invasion that, within the course of a few decades, of this new reign; under Norman, and later Swabian, rule, the town became a leading commercial power, the crossroads of Mediterranean trade during the age of the Crusades. Another foundation of Bari's prestige was the construction of the great basilica of San Nicola, which drew pilgrims from all over Europe.

Another coastal town that benefitted from Norman and Swabian rule was Trani, already a busy seaport under Byzantium. Trani's wealth and power is shown by its splendid cathedral, the abbey of Santa Maria di Colonna and other churches, and its handsome castle, built slightly later.

with white cliffs, while to the north it slopes down into hills and to the coastal lakes of Varano and Lesina. Offshore are the Tremiti islands, once a place of dreary banishment and ascetic monastic retreat. The surrounding seabeds abound in fish and underwater plants, and are now protected by a nature reserve. Just a few kilometres away as the crow flies, in the heart of the Gargano peninsula, mountain breezes turned Puglia over to the "men from the north," as skilled at politics as they were adroit with a sword. They soon established a single, powerful state where once only disarray and division had prevailed. In the next century or so, the region began to thrive. Building was undertaken, new towns were founded, and splendid Romanesque cathedrals became beacons for a new kind of urban society. Bari is a good example

Winds have shaped islands and coastlines into bizarre and intriguing shapes (preceding pages).

"Postcards" from Puglia: From "trulli" to worked stone and farm produce.

Let us take the fine view as an invitation to indulge in our curiosity as travellers. We could start from the Murge, exploring the blinding white centre of Ostuni, and then continue on to Martina Franca, a famed town of Baroque monuments. Then comes Alberobello, the town of the "trulli," curious round dwellings with whitewashed walls and conical roofs. Next we could head for the Salento, the Italian "heel," famous for its coastline and the Baroque splendour of Lecce. Heading west, we find mountainous

The story of Manfredonia is unique: the town was founded in 1256 by Manfred, a Swabian king, son and heir to Frederick II. He established the town that bore his name to house

San Leonardo di Siponto, with a richly ornamented portal. To complete this array of Romanesque magnificence, we should mention various other towns, each with a superb cathedral (Ruvo di

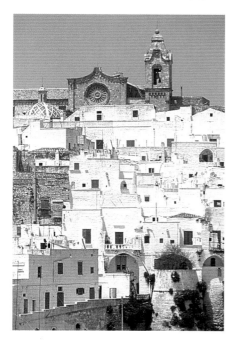

the inhabitants of Siponto, which had been largely destroyed by a catastrophic earthquake. Note the cathedral of Santa Maria di Siponto, a splendid Romanesque church, with square plan and central dome, clearly built in the eastern style, and the abbey church of

Puglia, Troia, Bitonto) and with other relics wrongly considered to be minor. To conclude this brief and partial tour of Norman and Swabian Puglia, we should mention a monument that marks the end of the Romanesque age, and the dawn of the Gothic age. The renowned Castel del Monte, built by emperor Frederick II, atop a solitary rise in the Murge hills. Although the architect is not known, some say that the emperor who ordered its construction also designed it. The spectacular view from the top of the castle encompasses most of the Murge and the plateau of the Tavoliere, extending as far as the Gargano and the Apennines.

Basilicata, a treasure chest of overlooked marvels. Among them, let us mention the massif of the Pollino, known for its ancient trees; the countryside, dotted with venerable old farmhouses; the coastline, which overlooks both the Ionian and the Tyrrhenian seas. Aside from the wonders of nature, Basilicata offers creations of man, as well: the "Sassi" of Matera, a series of grotto-homes, inhabited for thousands of years; or the Greek relics of Metaponto, or towns such as Potenza, Melfi, and Venosa, to name but a few, which together offer a traveller the key to a land still tied to its origins.

131

The Sky and Sea of the Tremiti Islands

Visible on the horizon from even the lower slopes of the Gargano promontory, the Tremiti islands – San Nicola, San Domino, and Capraia – stand just over twelve miles from the Italian shore. Inhabited since prehistoric times, they were known in ancient times as the "Rocks of Diomedes," from the legend of the Greek hero's burial here; Venus transformed his weeping companions into albatrosses (*Procellaria diomedea*), those broad-winged

Lombards against the Normans, later aiding their former Norman foes, and all the while dabbling in smuggling, in league with the pirates themselves. This free-and-easy behaviour finally brought down the wrath of the Holy See; in 1237 the corrupt monks were evicted, and replaced by a community of Cistercians. The island was fortified, but to no avail; the frustrated pirates managed to take the place by a ruse, and devastated the island. For many years the abbey was abandoned;

seabirds with a mournful cry, which still nest here. The Romans used the islands as a place of banishment for undesirables. Just after the year 1000, the Benedictine order founded an abbey – Santa Maria – here, building it on the dwellings of anchorites and early Christian churches. At first, the monks settled on the verdant San Domino; the island proved difficult to defend from pirate raids however. The monks moved to the nearby island of San Nicola, harsh but apparently impregnable. They built a monastery which soon became wealthy and powerful; the monks were cynical diplomats, supporting the Byzantines and

in 1412 monks of the Lateran order transformed the convent into a proper fortress, and restored and decorated the church. The abbey flourished anew; it even gained ownership of a large expanse of Pugliese coastline. Its wealth was abolished when the abbey was suppressed in the late

---

The clear waters of the "Rocks of Diomedes," which convey happiness and dispel every sad ancient legend.

The "architiello" of Capraia, a bridge built by sea and wind to reach the sky, and the utterly seductive and ancient island of San Nicola.

18th century; it was replaced by a penal colony, in use until the first decades of the 20th century.
Such is the history of this small archipelago, concentrated in the monumental ruins of San Nicola; the larger and more pleasant San Domino, instead, has become a modern tourist resort. The forbidding jagged cliffs of San Nicola contrast with the far more varied coastline of San Domino (nearly twice as long), with its odd and intriguing names (Crocodile Grotto, Elephant's Head, Cove of Little Roses, Beach of the Females, Falcon Cliff), all hinting at longer stays than in an ordinary island resort.

133

Frederick II: Emperor and, Perhaps, Architect

Frederick II was the son of Constance of Altavilla, the heiress of Sicily, and the emperor Henry VI, Barbarossa's son. He was a mighty warrior and statesman, as well as an original and fascinating thinker. He was as capable of razing a city that defied his authority as he was of endowing another city with magnificent new buildings. Under his rule, 13th-century Puglia enjoyed one of the most prosperous and enlightened periods in its history. Frederick considered this to be the pearl of his realm, and dwelt here often and at length; he ensured prosperity and thriving arts. This golden age left its mark in the form of many monuments: churches, cathedrals, mighty civic works, and above all military strongholds and fortifications, which the emperor intended as tangible signs of order under his rule. A network of castles extended across all of Puglia; many of them were older Norman or Byzantine castles, adapted to a square plan with a courtyard and corner towers. Castel del Monte offers an exception to this standard design. Built to a perfect, octagonal plan, this castle stands atop a sere hilltop of the Murge range. Faced with this remarkable structure in this remarkable site, one naturally wonders to what purpose it was built. It is thought to have been a hunting castle, set on the route of migratory birds; still, its symbolic impact is so clear and so powerful that it must underlie at least part of its design. This is a secular cathedral, a mighty crown of stone, meant to survey this land through centuries of imperial domination. The name of the architect is lost to memory. Some have hypothesized that Frederick himself may have designed it, but we have no evidence to support that belief. If the emperor himself did not plan

the castle, certainly we can say that it was designed in Frederick's court; no other setting in this part of Italy in this

The towers of Castel del Monte (facing page).

The massive bulk of the fortification stands on an isolated rise in the Murge.

Inside the castle, as well, the symbol of the octagon is a recurring motif.

period could have offered the intellectual and material resources for such a piece of architecture. At Frederick's court, one found the mathematical knowledge of Arabic scholars and Cistercian monks; the Apulian, or Pugliese, tradition of stone dressing; the tradition of classical art and architecture; and the new Gothic vitality that was percolating through the solemnity of the Romanesque. Architecturally, the castle has an eight-sided plan, with eight octagonal corner towers. Each facade is a solid curtain wall made of local limestone blocks; they were originally faced with marble slabs. The splendid portal is in the style of late antiquity. When Frederick II died in 1250, Puglia's period of prosperity came to an end, and this monument – symbolic of a golden age – suffered from neglect and decay. Used for many years as a prison, Castel del Monte was abandoned from the 18th century on. Stripped of its marble and its statues, it became a haven for shepherds, brigands, and political refugees. Finally, and happily, the newly founded Italian state restored the castle in 1876; from Andria or from Ruvo di Puglia, you can now drive up to admire this remarkable relic. 135

The Architectural Epic of the Cathedrals of Puglia

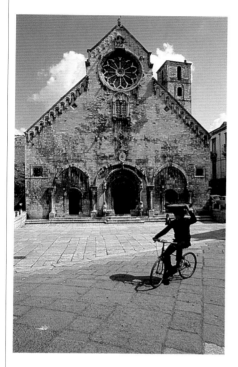

Following the grim centuries of the High Middle Ages, Puglia (or Apulia) – like much of the rest of Italy – experienced a period of religious and civic rebirth. Work proceeded, especially on great new cathedrals, and the new buildings were a workshop in which a new, Apulian Romanesque began to emerge. Further changes took place around 1220, when the Normans were ousted from power by the Swabians, under Frederick II. In the same period, we find the earliest traces

Cunning sculptures in the details of the cathedral of Trani (facing page).

The transition between Romanesque and Gothic at Ruvo di Puglia.

The cathedrals of Troia and Bitonto are joined in the memories of a composite artistic itinerary.

of the Gothic style; its soaring lines appeared in Romanesque cathedrals too, often rebuilt to the new style. A fine example of this is the cathedral of Bitonto, built between the late-12th and the early-13th centuries, in imitation of the basilica of San Nicola in Bari. This church is noteworthy for the harmony of its plan and its decoration. The facade features a superb rose window and an ornate portal; along the left side are six mullioned windows, each atop an arch. The interior, noble and severe in perfect Romanesque style, contains a noteworthy crypt, stretching beneath the length of the transept; attached to a pillar is the splendid ambo carved in 1229 by "Nicolaus sacerdos et magister" – Nicholas, priest and master craftsman. The Ruvo di Puglia cathedral, completed around 1237, was the product of a complex process of construction; it is indeed a Romanesque building, but it has a strong Gothic flavour. The facade has a sharply angled profile; a rose window fills much of the apex; the triple cornice and the archivolt of the central portal show lavish decoration. The magnificent and yet subdued interior reflects the soaring vertical lines of the facade.

The cathedral of Trani differs even more; built between the 12th and the mid-13th centuries, it is interesting for the mingling of Byzantine, Pisan, Lombard, and Amalfitan styles. It reveals a remarkable instance of stratification: at the lowest level is the hypogaeum of San Leucio (6th century); then, at the intermediate level are the church of Santa Maria della Scala (7th century) and the crypt of San Nicola (12th century); while a 13th-century Romanesque church is at the highest level. The facade has an elegant cuspidal pitch; note the fine rose window and the bronze portal by Barisano da Trani (1175-79). Last is the cathedral of Troia, built between 1093 and 1120; it shows Byzantine and Muslim influence. The splendid facade features a 13th-century rose window and a double bronze portal by Oderisio da Benevento (1119). The interior shows a typical basilican structure with a colonnade, and features fine artworks; note the fine sculpted pulpit (1169). These four monuments, all in the Terra di Bari and in the Capitanata, represent – in all their diversity – the complex history of Apulian Romanesque.

Past and Present Meet in the Sassi of Matera

Caves formed by erosion, ravines and sinkholes which drain away rainwater; here live plants and animals that survive in arid climates, as well as human beings who have become inured to the hardship of such harsh surroundings. These are the Murge hills, a limestone tableland that stretches from Puglia to the Basilicata. Ten thousand years ago, a community of shepherds settled here.

They may have been attracted by the yawning cavities in the cliff side, ideal the floor or balcony of the one above it; some ceilings even served to buttress public thoroughfares. Many churches were also hewn out of living rock. This, briefly, is the origin of Matera and its remarkable urban layout; the "Sassi" as they are known. A winding street runs through the two "rioni" or quarters of Matera. To the south is Sasso Caveoso, the more primitive of the two; to the north is Sasso Barisano, built more recently. Between them, on a spur, stands a Romanesque cathedral.

Following World War II, the Sassi were denounced as an unhappy landmark; hasty measures were taken, and the Sassi were evacuated. The inhabitants, willy-nilly, were moved to council houses in the new section of Matera. It took years before writers and scholars persuaded the government that its condemnation had been indiscriminate; in time, the remarkable quality of the Sassi earned recognition, and Unesco even designated them as part of the "heritage of humanity".

shelters for primitive man and his beasts, as well as by the relative abundance of water, supplied by a erratically flowing stream. Once all the natural caverns had been claimed and occupied, new ones were carved out. In time, humans learned to seal off the cave mouth with a wall; then, rooms were built, jutting outward, to enlarge the available living space. The dwellings, often set around a central courtyard, grew into a terraced town, where the roof of one home served as

All around stretches a maze of alleys and stairways, rife with uncommon sights and picturesque settings. The unsettling fascination of this town leads a visitor to wonder how so many came to live in this subterranean setting. It was less remarkable than it may seem to a modern visitor, back when the archaic economy, based on farming and livestock, was still the only alternative. With the advent of modernisation, this truly became a place of great squalor and misery.

Now 1,500 families have made a formal request to be allowed to return to live in the Sassi, after duly restoring them.

People have come back to live in the Sassi of Matera (facing page).

A little cliff-side church was carved out of the soft limestone of the Murge, particularly fit for carving and sculpture, suited to the courageous skill of those who climb up and work with it.

The Fanciful Splendour of Baroque Lecce

The province of Salento features a gently rolling landscape, with fertile red soil and occasional limestone outcroppings. The rock is finely grained and homogeneous; it is so soft that it can be shaped with adze, chisel, and hatchet. Once the rock is cut and shaped and set into place, however, it has a remarkable and highly valued property: it hardens and, in time,

acquires a warm golden hue. This excellent stone gave rise to a local craft tradition that, in later centuries, blossomed into a full-fledged art (16th-18th centuries). Lecce, the provincial capital, perhaps epitomizes this art. In those centuries, the artists of Lecce, while never forsaking the architectural style of Baroque, worked with an inexhaustible flair and tireless imagination, indulging their wildest

The rose window of the cathedral, a stunning piece of architectural composition (facing page).

A cherub, a spiral column, a complex festooned decoration: the sculptor's art is applied to the easily shaped stone that came from the local earth; this art and this stone gave Lecce its appearance.

flights of fancy in sculpted decorations, embellishing buildings with spiral columns, openwork balustrades, sumptuous cornices, lavish pediments, putti, and caryatids. This explosion of creativity, since it was the work of humble craftsmen rather than highly paid architects, quickly spread to the homes of the less prominent citizens as well; we can see intricately carved

window frames, sculpted balconies, doorways with ornamental borders, topped by heraldic devices.

It all beginning at the turn of the 17th century, when Lecce was radically rebuilt to satisfy the tastes of a new artistocracy of Spanish derivation, and to obey the dictates of the Counter Reformation. The clients and prime movers of this flourishing new art were a few powerful bishops, great religious orders, and wealthy local land-holding families. We also know who actually fashioned the wild and whimsical ornamentations in stone: master masons, contractors, and decorators; not architects. Around them must have worked great throngs of bricklayers, stone carvers, and craftsmen. These skilled workers kept the craft – or art, if you will – alive for three centuries. Lecce's earliest Baroque appears in the

basilica of Santa Croce, a fine example of the new style, and the adjacent Palazzo del Governo, or town hall. Dating from the 17th century is the spectacular town square, lined with some of Lecce's most remarkable buildings: the Duomo, or cathedral, with its magnificent bell tower, the Bishop's Palace, and the Seminary. Aside from Lecce's best-known monuments, however, the new style changed the face of the entire town, and spreading to ordinary streets and squares. The sumptuous, high-flown decoration of mansions and churches, originally meant to emphasize the power and wealth of a family or religious order, evolved into a collective and infectious phenomenon of astounding energy, rightly earning Lecce the sobriquet of the "Florence of the Baroque."

141

The Ancient World of Calabria and Sicily

A brilliant cerulean sky, the deep blue of the sea, the blinding yellow expanses of wheat, broken here and there by the pallid green of almond trees, the mighty shapes of ancient temples: these are the basic elements of one of the most classic and Apollonian aspects of Sicily, unchanged since ancient Greek colonists first called this land Trinacria (after its three-pointed shape), part of ancient Magna Graecia.

Before you explore Sicily, however, you may wish to explore Calabria, a land rich in tradition and history, set at the northwestern tip of the Italian peninsula. Here, you can admire the collections of ancient Greek art and artifacts in the Museo Nazionale in Reggio di Calabria; here you can see the "Bronzes of Riace," two celebrated statues found in the waters off Calabria several decades ago, and now stunningly restored. After crossing the Strait of Messina, you can enjoy the

Sicilian landscape and sunshine until you reach the famous Valley of Temples at Agrigento; here Doric colonnades still stand, perfectly harmonizing with the surrounding landscape. The landscape is similar if not identical at Selinunte, but the temples lie scattered in dramatic ruins, overturned by war and earthquake. Fate was kinder to the

theatre and temple of Segesta, a roofless enclosure where 25 centuries ago sacrifices were made to the cult of the local deity. Yet a different destiny was reserved for the Phoenician town of Mozia; this was a prosperous town of the extreme western tip of Sicily, surrounded by a lagoon. After its destruction by the Syracusans, the survivors founded on nearby Capo Lilibeo the first settlement of what was one day to become Marsala; archeologists even now are trying to recreate their city, 2,000 years later. Then comes the exuberant town of Palermo, surrounded by palm trees and holm oaks. The constant sound of flowing water, the buildings with their reddish domes, the exquisite decorations – these are the ingredients of yet another aspect of Sicily, younger

The impressive temple of Concordia in the Valley of Temples near Agrigento (preceding pages).

Capo Colonna, in Calabria.

A detail of the spectacular Baroque of Villa Palagonia in Bagheria, near Palermo.

The Norman cathedral stands out over Cefalù and the blue waters of the sea.

by a thousand years than the first setting we described. This image should take us back to the transition from Moorish to Norman culture; a transition that, even after a 30-year war of conquest, occurred without excessive rancour or strife. This was the result of the intelligent Norman policy of involving all the diverse communities on the island in the administration of the new state. After this 11th-century conquest, Sicily – endowed by nature with its strategic location at the heart of the Mediterranean, and now guided by a powerful and active monarchy – reinforced its traditional role as middleman between West and East, between Christendom and the Levant. Trade thrived and soon wealth or at least prosperity was widespread. Palermo once again stood as a leading Mediterranean port; this led to a remarkable flowering of the arts and sciences. Many major buildings were renovated or reconstructed; vast gardens were planted. This period witnessed the creation of many other landmarks and monuments of a newly and uniquely prosperous Sicily. On the fringes of the Conca d'Oro, Palermo's rich agriculturaly plain, in the small village of Monreale, William II of Sicily ordered the construction of a great cathedral in 1174. With its adjacent Benedictine monastery, Monreale is a remarkable blend of diverse architectural styles,

a splendid example of the golden age of Romanesque sculpture in Sicily (note the capitals of the slender columns in the cloister). Much the same thing happened at Cefalù, a harbour town on the slopes of a promontory overlooking the Tyrrhenian coast. Here, the Norman conquest brought a period of wealth and superb artistic creation that led to the building of the renowned cathedral of Cefalù. Unfinished though it is, this cathedral is still one of the finest pieces of religious architecture of its time. It is embellished with a vast and exquisite series of Byzantine-style mosaics. Yet another aspect is to be found in Tindari, a town built by the Syracusans and then destroyed by the Moors, looming over the blue sea and fine sands beneath. Or consider Erice, an ancient town atop a hill near Trapani and its vast plain. Erice was a major centre under Moorish rule, and it grew more important under the Normans, who enlarged the walls and built a castle here. Today, Erice is largely intact, and visitors here feel as if they had been swept back in time. And Sicily offers other images still: different shapes, different colours, steeped in the Baroque or in other, more recent cultures and times.

Look at the villas of Bagheria, near Palermo; head east, to Mount Etna and cities such as Messina, Catania, Syracuse, and Taormina, to name only the best known. Limitations of space prevent us from exploring Sicily as we should, completing our virtual circuit around the island.

The Greek theatre of Segesta, ancient town of the Elimi, and a solemn reminder of bygone ages.

The sands of Tindari seem to be encroaching upon the sea, in search of the horizon.

Salt flat near Marsala, a city founded by Phoenicians.

Treasures from the Sea in Reggio di Calabria

The shipwreck was probably caused by a terrible storm. Whatever it was that sank an ancient galley off the coast of Riace in the Ionian Sea twenty long centuries ago, it was a blessed event for archeologists. Perhaps those archeologists can be forgiven for gloating over an event that certainly resulted in loss of life. After all, the cargo of this particular galley was not a load of common amphorae or food. Instead, that fateful Roman ship was transporting two masterpieces of 5th-century B.C. Greek sculpture, two of the very few bronzes that survive from that remarkable period of history. Just why these great sculptures were being shipped is unknown to us. Perhaps they were plunder of war, taken from glorious Athens by the new Roman conquerors, and sent back to the homeland to adorn the villa of some

powerful senator. Perhaps they were being sent back East, as the capital of the Empire was being shifted from Rome to Constantinople. We can be practically certain, however, of the subjects portrayed here. They were two athletes, the winners of the Athenian "hoplitodromia," i.e., a foot race run in a full suit of armour. First held in 520 B.C., and run until well into the Hellenistic age, these races were hotly contested. Victory, after all, meant enormous honour. Statues of the winners were erected in the most visible place in Athens. In support of this interpretation, let us consider the poses of the two powerful figures: the left arm is bent to hold a shield, there are marks on the head indicating a helmet, and the right hand is clenched, perhaps to grasp a weapon. The shields, helmets, and spears – admittedly hypothetical – have in any case been lost, somewhere on the seabed. It is easy to imagine the astonishment of the divers who first glimpsed these magnificent artworks in the underwater muck and darkness, in August 1972. Covered with encrustations, but clearly masterpieces of Greek art, the "Bronzes of Riace," as they immediately came to be known, were

handed over for restoration. For nine long years, they remained hidden from public view. The patina of time and water was patiently and carefully removed. Now it was possible to appreciate fully both the skill with which they were cast and the cloisonné that adorned lips, teeth, and nipples. The unveiling was a major Italian event: the two statues, gleaming after their restoration, have now found their most fitting location in the Museo Nazionale of Reggio di Calabria.

The "Bronzes of Riace" have preserved their stern and confident gazes and all of their original allure (facing page).

The Museo Nazionale houses major artifacts and finds from all over Calabria and Basilicata, dating back to prehistory in some cases.

The Norman-Moorish Heritage of Palermo

"The island of Sicily is the pearl of the century, the first land on earth in abundance of nature, and antiquity of civilization... Foremost among its cities is Palermo, and if one were to list that town's fine qualities, one could never make an end of it... It lies on the shores of the sea and is surrounded by mighty and lofty mountains... Its buildings are so handsome that travellers set off from great distances, drawn by the renown of the wonders of Palermo's architecture..." This remarkable passage is by Edrisi, an Arabic geographer who settled at the court of Roger II, the first Norman king of Sicily. We can certainly imagine that the Islamic scholar may have wished to compliment his tolerant sovereign, but the description that he gives of Palermo at the dawn of the second millennium is not far from reality. With the Norman conquest, in 1072, the city of Palermo underwent a radical transformation. The old Moorish castle was transformed into a palace, glittering with mosaics, for the new monarchs. The Norman kings created vast pleasure parks dotted with mansions, pavillions, fountains, and fishponds; a few remarkable ruins survive. Within the walls of Palermo itself, the work of renovation was chiefly directed toward the various churches – San Giovanni degli Eremiti, the cathedral, the Martorana, San Cataldo, and others. These churches are utterly distinctive: cubic volumes topped with hemispherical domes, reddish in hue against the backdrop of green-and-yellow palm trees; they feature braided arches and complex open-work, splendid mosaics with glittering gold backgrounds. All these mixtures and blends are the clear demonstration of an admirable and remarkably effective policy of tolerance. As the government of the new conquerors was asking all communities of the island – Latins, Greeks, Jews, and Muslims – to work together, it was pure wisdom to ease the trauma of occupation. Almost as an afterthought, this allowed the gradual development of the cultural seeds planted in earlier periods.

The exterior of the cathedral almost seems to be filigree made by a fine jeweller (facing page).

Red, but faded by the Sicilian sunshine, are the domes of San Cataldo.

Little columns at San Giovanni degli Eremiti and in the bell tower of the Martorana – lightness attained.

Light and Colour in the Cathedral of Monreale

After Sicily was conquered by the Normans in the 11th century, the island enjoyed a period of relative peace and prosperity, under a strong and active new monarchy. Sicily was thus able to reinforce its strategic position in the central Mediterranean, and strengthen its role as middleman between Europe and the Levant, a role that was fundamental to Sicilian prosperity and power. Following the 30-year war of conquest, trade resumed quickly, and money flowed into the coffers of the cities of the island kingdom. Messina and Palermo were once again leading ports of the Mediterranean Sea; in both cities there was a great flowering of the arts and sciences, and splendid buildings were erected. During this period, great changes were made in both cities' appearance and layout, and several major churches were founded, such as the cathedrals of Cefalù and Monreale. The purpose behind the building of these new churches was to bring Christianity to parts of the island that had become profoundly Islamic. In the case of Monreale, the new cathedral and monastery – around which a town sprang up in due time – was set at the edge of the fertile plain that extends inland from Palermo, known as the Conca d'Oro. Under Moorish rule, a small farming village stood here. To proselytize, the Norman king of Sicily, William II, summoned a community of Benedictine monks. They took up residence in the vast complex, which included a splendid cathedral, the Archbishop's Palace, and a royal residence. The cathedral itself is a remarkable building; Islamic, Byzantine, and Romanesque influence can all be detected in the architecture. It is certainly one of the masterpieces of mediaeval Italy.

The influence of North Italian Romanesque can be seen in the twin towers that frame the facade, while the basilican layout is an evident Romanesque feature. Islamic influence can be clearly seen in the spectacular motif of braided arches running around the exterior of the apses; note the striking contrast between the light-coloured limestone and the black volcanic stone. The Byzantine style appears in the series of mosaics with gold background in the aisles, chapels, sanctuary, and apses; the mosaics cover a total of 6,340 square metres. These mosaics are an important document. They recount a complete history of the Christian religion, from the Bible stories to the lives of Sicilian saints. There are even scenes of the Sicilian king at prayer; he is shown dressed in the garb of an Eastern monarch, presenting this same church as an offering to Jesus and the Virgin Mary. Equally spectacular is the celebrated cloister of the Benedictine monastery. In particular, note the graceful portico, clearly Moorish in construction. There are 26 Moorish arches and 228 slender twin columns, covered with mosaic inlay and carved into arabesques. In a corner enclosure, there is a remarkable fountain shaped like a palm tree.

The decorations envelop the architecture in fancy (facing page).

The exterior is a lovely chest for the treasures contained within.

The cloister, with twin columns and little Romanesque capitals; a detail of the mosaics that glitter in the cathedral.

151

The Greek Temples of Sicily

"They eat as if they were going to die tomorrow, and they build as if they were going to live forever" – the Agrigento-born philosopher Empedocles wrote these words in the 5th century B.C. to describe his fellow Sicilians. Perhaps the humour is a bit cutting, but it nicely describes the limitless ambitions of the Greek colonists in Sicily at that time. Just three centuries had passed since the first Greek settlers had landed on the Sicilian coasts, and the colonies had already multiplied, breaking off and spreading westward and inland. Both the Phoenicians of nearby Carthage and the Athenians in the motherland had done their best to throttle the infant nation in its crib, so to speak. The Greek colonists, however, defeated the Carthaginians in 480 B.C. at Himera.

The chariot of Apollo, one of the metopes of Temple C at Selinunte (facing page).

The Temple of Hercules in the Valley of Temples at Agrigento.

Temple E, at Selinunte, reassembled where parts collapsed.

The powerful solemnity of the unfluted columns of the Doric temple of Segesta.

They went on to thrash an Athenian fleet at Syracuse in 413 B.C. During the 5th century, the Greek colonies of Magna Graecia extended their trading contacts, and began to accumulate the sort of wealth that was needed to construct the great Doric temples that we can still admire in Agrigento, Selinunte and Segesta, the splendid heritage of a golden age. Pindar described Agrigento as "the loveliest city inhabited by mortals"; the city was founded around 580 B.C. A century later it had extended its rule over a great portion of Sicily. Agrigento was so wealthy that it was able to build all the temples that now grace the valley south of town during the same time. Selinunte is the westernmost Greek colony in Sicily. It was founded by Greek city of Megara Hyblaea in 628 B.C. Selinunte had a spectacular rise and an equally meteoric decline. At first the city established good relations with the nearby and powerful Carthage; then Selinunte contracted an alliance with Syracuse. As it expanded northward, in search of access to the Tyrrhenian Sea, Selinunte found a mortal enemy in Segesta, the most important city of the Elimi. Segesta is best known now for its enormous temple, remarkably complete, in a stunning setting. In one of Segesta and Selinunte's frequent conflicts, Segesta called on Carthage for help; the Carthaginians sent an army of 100,000 men. Selinunte was defeated when reinforcements from Syracuse and Agrigento failed to arrive in time. Selinunte saw 16,000 of its inhabitants slain outright; 5,000 deported; the remainder scattered to the four winds. Its renowned temples were abandoned; an earthquake later reduced them to the magnificent ruin that so impressed travellers in the 19th century.

The Nature and Traditions of Sardini

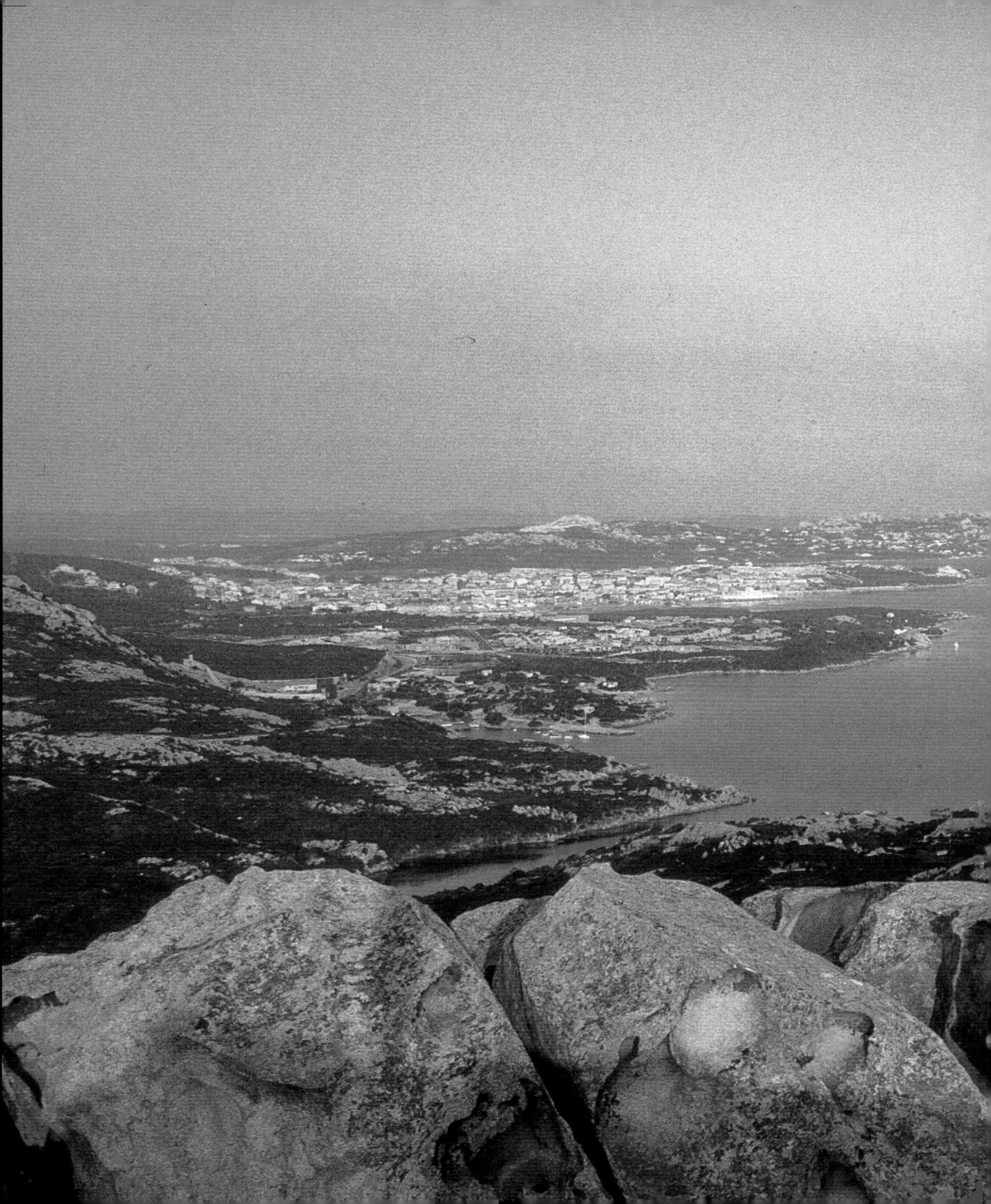

The Nature and Traditions of Sardinia

Greetings from the Costa Smeralda! Postcards carry these words, but no postcard could do justice to the "Emerald Coast." The sea here is an iridescent palette ranging from cobalt blue to the intense green that gives it its name. The coastline is an endless embroidery of weather-worn granite. The vegetation inland – Mediterranean underbrush known as the "maquis" – is a shifting array of colours. The brilliant sunshine tans the limbs of the rich and famous. Everywhere are discreet but luxurious villas, exclusive shopping streets, vintage sailboats, and enormous yachts. At least, that is the image that many have of Sardinia. They do not know that the Costa Smeralda, lovely as it most assuredly is, consists of only a narrow strip of shoreline, blessed with a sudden shower of money from tourists and holidays. The coast has been catapulted from hundreds of years of subsistence economy and shepherding to the fast lane of modern consumer culture. You don't have to go far from the artificial paradise of holiday-makers and VIPs to discover many facets of an

island that for centuries was closed off to the rest of the world, developing its own inimitable culture, then becoming an occupied territory, seeing the ships of many different conquerors touching at its harbours. Each new arrival shaped the local culture and personality, but was in turn shaped by them.

Consider Alghero, a port town founded by Genoa in 1102, and then occupied, over the course of the late 14th century, by the Spanish. The old town, where the lively dialect of Catalonian colonists is still spoken, is virtually intact; the ramparts that overlook the waterfront give us a precise image of

Alghero's centuries as a seaside citadel. Lovely and unique, the town is bounded to the south by the long and rugged coast road that leads to Bosa, and to the north by the Roman town of Porto Torres and the cliffs of Capo Caccia, home to the last surviving griffon vultures. Another remarkable area, in

Rock carved by the tireless ministrations of nature at Capo d'Orso, near Palau (preceding pages).

The surprising hues of the sea in the paradisiacal archipelago of the Maddalena.

Wild horses in a pristine setting.

A traditional outfit at Oristano.

the centre of the northern coastline, is the Anglona; the capital city of this zone is Castelsardo. Naturally fortified, atop a great promontory, this town preserves the ancient structure of the mighty Genoan stronghold. Inland and to the south, beyond the fertile valley, lies an amphitheatre of rocks, carved into bizarre shapes by the strong sea breezes; this stony setting is made even more evocative by the presence of prehistoric funerary temples, actually hewn into some of the largest and most dramatic boulders. Inland, and

especially in the area around Logudoro, there is a remarkable array of Romanesque churches. They were largely built between 1000 and 1300, in styles borrowed from various mainland schools of architecture, but principally in the Pisan style. These churches are the heritage of communities of monks who were trying to render these lands fruitful. The most spectacular single landmark here is the church of the

Santissima Trinità di Saccargia, not far from Sassari. At the same time, Logudoro, with the neighbouring territory of Meilogu, contains a great abundance of ruins and relics of one of the most significant cultures of the prehistoric Mediterranean. The Valley of the Nuraghi – this term has been used to

describe the area south of Torralba, studded with "nuraghi" megalithic structures shaped like a truncated cone; some stand alone, while some others are exceedingly complex , full-fledged "palaces" ringed by walls and with an entourage of lesser "nuraghi." We should also mention the Gallura, a region of uninhabited mountains and highlands, in the economic sphere of the Costa Smeralda. Here too you need only emerge from the rectangular frame of the postcard to discover a different world: towns like Santa Maria Gallura, once an outpost of the House of Savoy, and now a fishing village famed for its intricately worked coral and its handsome beaches; splendid settings such as the granite-bound Capo Testa, which served as a quarry for Roman temples; unrivalled sailing off the windy archipelago of the Maddalena; and remarkable islands like Caprera. Then there would be... In fact, if you let your eye wander over the map, you will see the massif of the Gennargentu, a wildlife and nature preserve, as well as the heartland of the most genuine ancient pastoral culture of Sardinia. And then there is the area around Cagliari and the southern coast, a place of fine art and spectacular scenery. There is no end to the array of opportunities; the only thing that we can be sure of, unfortunately, is that we will have certainly left out many of the excellent reasons to travel to Sardinia, and explore its varied and fascinating lands.

Lunette and frieze of the cathedral of Santa Maria, in Cagliari.

The waves break and foam sprays on the coast near Castelsardo.

The "Navicella," a bronze from the same culture as the "nuraghi."

The Rescued Lands between Cagliari and the Sulcis

Among the many wonders of nature found in Sardinia, one of the most spectacular is the Sulcis, on the SW tip of the island. Abounding in remarkable views and exotic species of wildlife, this rocky area slopes down into the sea, forming two large islands, Sant'Antioco and San Pietro, and a succession of jagged promontories and bays. Inhabited since prehistoric times, as the numerous "nuraghi" demonstrate, the Sulcis was later

colonized by Phoenician settlers. They founded the city of Sulcis – whose name has been applied to the area at large – and introduced grain as a crop. The Sulcis was a prosperous agricultural province under Roman rule, too – a breadbasket of the Empire – but when the Empire declined and fell, it was sacked and plundered by Vandals and Saracens. It was not until the 16th century that the Sulcis was repopulated by communities that survived by herding, as they still do. In recent years, following a brief foray into mining, the

Sulcis is looking to tourism as the principal resource on which to base its future development.
You can reach this remarkable area from Cagliari; it is a short drive, and it begins in a truly spectacular fashion. You pass through the area of ponds just inland from town, where thousands of birds live in total safety. The unrivalled king of these brackish expanses is the flamingo. Long a wayfarer, stopping over in Sardinia during the yearly migration southward, the flamingo has recently established a permanent colony here, truly an unusual event in the Mediterranean.
Another hour of driving will take you into the heart of a wild and almost entirely uninhabited massif. Among the granite slopes is concealed a complex of maquis and forest that extends from north to south for nearly 30 kilometres. There is only one road fit for cars. Along the steep watercourses, stands

of oleanders alternate with dark groves of alders. In the maquis there are tall bunches of heather and brier, arbutus trees, and myrtle, fighting for domination against holm oaks – which attain spectacular sizes – and families of rough-barked cork trees. This forest primeval is one of the last "sanctuaries" of the Sardinian stag.

Flamingos near Cagliari (facing page).

Flowering euphorbias near Capo Malfatano.

Intricate rock formations overlook the wind-tossed inland of the island.

Deer in the preserve of Monte Arcosu, a major protected area of the WWF.

The Times of Man in Ancient Tharros

The strategic role played by Sardinia in antiquity was clearly that of tactical base to support maritime trade. Mycaenean, Cypriot, and Phoenician sailors all had ports here, but only the Phoenicians settled here permanently, in the 8th century B.C. The ancient trading ports of the SW coast thus became the nuclei of Phoenician cities: *Karalis*, which is now Cagliari; Nora; Sulcis; and Tharros, to name only the most important.

Tharros was founded around the year 800 B.C. on a spit of land that offered two different anchorages, in the consolidated tradition of Phoenician harbours.

Later, under the Carthaginians, Tharros was a major maritime stronghold controlling the western Mediterranean and the routes to *Massalia* (Marseilles). In 238 B.C. it fell into Roman hands; during the Byzantine era it was an episcopal see and a fortress, but in the 8th and 9th centuries it was abandoned, following Saracen raids.

The location of the city was known as early as the 16th century, and the earliest excavations – carried out in pursuit of rich but illusory troves of gold – triggered an ongoing treasure hunt that ended only in the 19th century. More recent excavations by archeologists determined that the ancient seaport stood on three low hills on the little peninsula: the ring of walls was largely oval in layout; the town was uncovered, in its three phases (Phoenician, Carthaginian, and

Roman); the area of temples and necropolises came to light.

Of particular importance was the discovery of the "tophet," the sanctuary of Phoenician and Carthaginian deities in which the firstborn males of the city's aristocracy were sacrificed each year. We can still see the layout of the town along the main street, lined with homes and shops.

Among the material found in the Museo Archeologico di Cagliari, note the various terracotta "masks," one of the most distinctive products of the artists of Tharros, with their unbroken contacts with the Carthaginian world.

The Corinthian columns overlooking the sea date from the reign of Caesar (facing page).

Residential centres and cisterns, wide basalt roads with sewers: Tharros clearly features considerable historical stratification of the human settlement on the peninsula in the Gulf of Oristano.

A satyr's mask from the Punic period.

The Ancient Stones of Sardinia

A particularly appropriate symbol for the proud island of Sardinia, the "nuraghi" are mighty stone towers of venerable antiquity. Over the centuries, all sorts of theories have been set forth as to their original functions – temples of the sun, mausoleums, fortresses – as well as their builders. Now we know enough to laugh at some of those suppositions, but there is much we still do not understand: without a doubt, the "nuraghi" were a combination of residence of the head of the tribe and a structure for the defense of the community in case of attack. The oldest ones date from the early Bronze Age and stand alone; later "nuraghi" date from the earliest period of Phoenician settlement. These are multiple structures; they are ringed by enclosure walls like full-fledged castles. Often, they were surrounded by extensive and maze-like villages; some of the larger villages had as many as 200 huts. All of these features are indications of the considerable progress achieved by a society of farmers and herders that was

certainly one of the most advanced in the Mediterranean basin. Though this civilization was restricted to the island of Sardinia, it had a great and complex history. While the "nuraghi" are the most visible relics of ancient Sardinia, there are also notable monuments to the ancient Sardinian religion. Handsome bronze statuettes have been found, one of the finest relics of Sardinian civilization. Equally distinctive are the "tombs of the giants," enormous collective sepulchres comprising a

massive stele, with a doorway into the tomb, and an enclosure of broad stone slabs, marking off the area dedicated to the cult. Alongside them, often, we find remarkable carved stones, oval in shape, the so-called "betili" marked with symbols of the fundamental principle of the universe – masculine and feminine – found in ancient naturalistic religions. Lastly, there are the "Domus de Janas," or "witches' houses," funerary loculi carved into a broad array of surfaces. Some of them are small and cramped, others are large and well decorated. Occasionally, they are carved into the rock formations in the interior uplands that the wind has worn into fantastic shapes.

Seen from inside, the "nuraghe" of Santu Antine reveals its structure (facing page).

The "betili," objects of the fertility cult.

A flock grazes around the "nuraghe" of Santu Antine.

The giant's tomb of Coddhu 'Ecchiu.

The Solitary Masterpiece of Saccargia

Sardinia, as we all know well, is a land of surprises. The enigmatic "nuraghe" with its enigmatic counterparts, the necropolis and the underground sanctuary; the flame-coloured flamingos that crowd the ponds of Cagliari and Oristano; the eerie granite shapes modelled by the winds along the north coast. Joining these singular phenomena is a less well known group of Romanesque churches that stand in the solitary landscape inland from Sassari. Particularly rife in these structures are the lands of Logudoro, which have for millennia been the crossroads of the great arteries of communication between Sardinia's leading seaports: Cagliari, Porto Torres, and Olbia. As you cross this zone, what is most impressive is the isolation of the churches. Far from the major cities, this is a natural feature of the environment that only enhances their magnificence. Still, the solitude of the Pisan-Romanesque churches in Sardinia is not a product of chance; rather it is the result of specific historical circumstances. These churches, in fact, date from the first three centuries after the year 1000, a time in which local lords tried to make their barren lands more fruitful by encouraging the introduction of monastic communities that had previously "redeemed" so to speak, other unhealthy sections of the mainland. The monks who came here from all over Italy, but especially from the area around Pisa, brought with them

The Santissima Trinità of Saccargia, an example of the Pisan-Romanesque style in Sardinia (facing page).

A view of the porch and a 13th-century fresco.

the industriousness of the faithful, as well as a series of practical concepts which were the more solid practical foundations of a Romanesque church. The forms and decorations that came

with these monks were developed over time, resulting in an original Sardinian version of colour and embellishment, in some cases quite daring and advanced. Along the island roads, then, a true atlas of the Romanesque style was set forth; the most spectacular page was certainly that of the church of the Santissima Trinità of Saccargia. This building, founded in 1116, still reveals the distinctive appearance given it by the Pisan master craftsmen who worked on it, from 1180 to 1200. Before it is a three-arched porch; the front has alternating black-and-white bands. The interior is stern, austere, embellished only by the great series of frescoes in the apse. One interesting note: the word "Saccargia" apparently means "the dappled cow" a reference that at first glance might seem irreverent. Apparently, however, the name derives from an actual, dappled cow that would miraculously genuflect, offering its milk to the friars on the rise where they would later build the church.

From Gilded Leisure to the Voices of the Winds

Costa Smeralda, or Emerald Coast – those two words are quite sufficient to conjure up one of the most prosperous tourist resorts in all of Italy. It deserves its considerable fame; any attempt to explain the attractions of this sun-kissed shoreline tends to slip into superlatives and high-flown metaphors. As a result, the Costa Smeralda has become a modern myth. All the same, it is hard not to sing its praises: the water here actually does cover the entire palette of blues, from cobalt to aquamarine to azure; the shoreline really is a succession of giant arabesques carved out of the granite cliffs by wind and water; and inland you really do find scenes of pastoral beauty and bucolic enchantment.

In the face of such idyllic loveliness, the visitor just has to marvel at what an earthly paradise this must have been no more than fifty years ago, when only monk seals sunned themselves on the beaches, and the only sails cutting the perfect horizon were the lateen sails of little vessels working the coasting trade. The Costa Smeralda, then, is unquestionably a splendid setting. It has, as backdrop, a hinterland of remarkable beauty. It has as accessories, shall we say, the creations of man. Whatever else we may say, the development has been undertaken with admirable restraint, in a style that is well suited to the setting.

Not far from these beaches of gold-plated leisure, and the surrounding playgrounds of the rich and their admirers, there are other areas of Sardinia, quieter, less sybaritic, more natural. Take, for example, the archipelago of the Maddalena; arid, jagged, and swept by the cold northerly mistral. These islands are splendid granite sculptures, softened by the expanses of aromatic herbs and the dense Mediterranean maquis; the realm of cormorants and peregrine falcons, surrounded by seabeds abounding in fish and underwater plants. This is a harsh environment that captured the heart of Giuseppe Garibaldi, the man who brought about Italian unification. In 1849, following the disastrous attempt to liberate Rome, he came here, landing on the island of Caprera. And after Italy was well and truly united in 1870, Garibaldi returned here, and spent his remaining years as a farmer and island-dweller.

An inlet on the island of Mortorio, not far from the Costa Smeralda (facing page).

Little bays and islets, shoals that can be explored underwater, and the occasional beach, where you can take the sun.

The elite dock at Porto Cervo, while the Mediterranean maquis offers romantic little nooks to one and all.